The Public Librarian's Guide to the Internet

The Public Librarian's Guide to the Internet

Sally Criddle

UK Office for Library and Information Networking

Alison McNab

Pilkington Library, Loughborough University

Sarah Ormes

UK Office for Library and Information Networking

Ian Winship

Learning Resources Department,
University of Northumbria at Newcastle

Published in association with the UK Office for Library and Information Networking, University of Bath

Library Association Publishing
London

Published by
Library Association Publishing
7 Ridgmount Street
London WC1E 7AE

Library Association Publishing is wholly owned by The Library Association.

First published 2000

British Library Cataloguing in Publication Data

A catalogue record for this book is available from the British Library.

ISBN 1-85604-328-2

UKOLN is jointly funded by Resource: the Council for Museums, Archives and Libraries and by the Joint Information Systems Committee of the Higher Education Funding Councils (JISC). It also receives project funding from the European Union and support from the University of Bath. More information about UKOLN and its activities can be found at **http://www.ukoln.ac.uk/**

Typeset from authors' disk in 11/14 Elegant Garamond by Library Association Publishing.
Printed and made in Great Britain by MPG Books Ltd, Bodmin, Cornwall.

Contents

The authors

Sally Criddle MSc is Resource Coordinator for UKOLN, the UK Office for Library and Information Networking.

Alison McNab MA MSc MIInfSc ALA is Academic Services Manager, Pilkington Library, Loughborough University.

Sarah Ormes MA is Public Library Networking Focus for UKOLN, the UK Office for Library and Information Networking.

Ian Winship BA MA ALA is Electronic Services Manager, Learning Resources Department, University of Northumbria at Newcastle.

Introduction

The Internet is going to revolutionize public libraries. Already it allows even the smallest branch library to access hundreds of databases from all around the world. It allows the children's librarian to provide users with up-to-the-minute pictures from the latest NASA mission. It allows the family history librarian to access genealogical databases from around the world. It allows the reference librarian to look up phone numbers from Argentina and search patent directories from the USA. It allows librarians themselves to learn easily from the experiences of other librarians and libraries around the world. The Internet is impacting on all areas of public library services and will affect all staff. The library in the public's mind will soon no longer be simply a place to borrow a book, find the answer to a question or use as a place to study. Libraries will be seen as access points to the Internet, IT training organizations and mediators to a wealth of online information. People's expectations of public libraries could change rapidly and so librarians need to quickly develop awareness not just of what the Internet is, but also of how it can be integrated into the library's services. From the Saturday morning assistant to the Chief Librarian the ability to surf the Net, to help a user telnet to their e-mail account and to help a child find the *Dancing Hamsters* page (**http://www.hamsterdance.com/**) will be crucial.

This book is designed to help people survive this revolution, to become enthused by the new world it is creating and to get involved! It has been written to help manage the provision of online services on a day-to-day basis and to de-mystify the Internet. The book is not a technical manual but a practical guide. It aims to show that the Internet is just a tool to be used to improve and extend public library services.

The book is divided into three main sections. The first section explores exactly what the Internet is, how it works and how it can best be exploited. It provides basic tips on what an Internet address is and how it works. Essential online communication skills will be identified and explained. E-mail, discussion groups, newsgroups and basic netiquette will all be discussed in a public library context. Chapters 5 (on searching) and 6 (on browsing) provide tips on how to make sense of the chaos of the Internet and make it work for you. By the end of this section the reader will have a basic grounding in the skills required to use the Internet successfully. Even the least confident surfer will know the difference between the web and the Internet and between a newsgroup and a mailing list after reading this section.

The second section of the book is a guide to some of the best resources available on the Internet. It can be used as a directory to help answer those difficult reference questions or simply as a way of getting to grips with the kind of information and services available on the Internet. Resources about public libraries and professional development are highlighted here. The lists of resources are not exhaustive, but aim to indicate the type of resources available. As with all Internet books some of the resources listed will move, disappear or simply cease to be updated. However, at the time of writing all resources listed were valid and current.

Practically all the information resources referred to in this book are available for free. Commercial databases typically remain a charged-for service, but resources like recent back issues of newspapers, the entire *Encyclopedia Britannica* and an increasing number of previously expensive government papers are now available for free online. The Internet extends the range of resources the public library can offer its users both physically and financially.

The directory is divided into different chapters which are then again subdivided, allowing useful sites to be found quickly. Where possible individual sites have also been annotated with their strengths or weaknesses highlighted.

The final section of the book explores issues about integrating the Internet into public library services. Information is given about developing public library websites and useful web resources are listed. Ideas are offered about the kind of online services public libraries could develop and examples are provided. The book's aim is not to be exhaustive, but simply to provide ideas, raise awareness about possibilities and provide guidance on where more detailed information can be found.

The final chapter in the book looks forward to what the next few years of Internet services in public libraries are going to bring. It highlights the possible outcomes of current UK Government initiatives and tries to identify future Internet trends that public librarians need to be aware of now. The book closes with a glossary which explains the technical terms and acronyms used throughout the book.

The Internet provides an opportunity for public libraries to revolutionize what they do and how they do it. The integration of the Internet into library services is a personal challenge to every public librarian. We all need to learn new skills, spot new opportunities and deal with a constant tide of change and technical development. It is hoped that this book will in some small way make this revolution less painful.

Part 1

The basics

1

What is the Internet and how can it help you and your library?

- ★ Background
- ★ Access to the Internet
- ★ Statistics and demographics
- ★ What you will and won't find on the Internet

During the 1990s the Internet caught the public imagination in a way few other technologies have done. Over this period access for the whole of society has moved from being restricted to a few sectors (higher education and larger companies) in the early 1990s to an estimated 26–56% of the total population of the UK having online access by early 2000. In the past year, advertisements for e-commerce sites have become common in all forms of the media and the growth of Internet-only companies (increasingly called *dot.com* companies) such as *Amazon.com* (worth $20bn in January 2000) represents one aspect of the e-commerce revolution.

So what is the Internet? Well, contrary to what some have said, it is not – yet – the greatest information source ever with the answers to all your questions. In essence, the Internet is an international network of computer networks – it links millions of computers around the world, and can be used for many different and ever-growing purposes. The Internet allows users to access different types of information (for example, documents and software) as if they were held on your own computer, and other people can read documents you choose to 'publish' on the Internet as if they were held on their own machine.

This book discusses two main ways in which you can use the Internet: to communicate with other people, and to find information.

Communication can take the form of using electronic mail to correspond with a range of individuals or groups. Your correspondents may be your colleagues working in the same organization (whether in the same building or a different location) or library users who have e-mailed requests and enquiries. You may also be assisting users to communicate with family and friends in other cities or countries, or individuals from around the world who share their enthusiasm for a particular author or involvement in a self-help group. It can also consist of publishing your CV, a creative writing project, or factual information on the world wide web (see Chapter 3).

The sort of information which can be located on the Internet is extremely wide-ranging. Chapters 5 and 6 describe complementary ways of searching for information.

Background

The Internet as we know it today developed from an experimental computer network in the USA in the early 1970s. Standard techniques enable different types of computer running different software to talk to one other and exchange data (information), so forming the seamless network that we know today as the Internet. The information that you send to other people (perhaps as an electronic mail message), or that someone requests from a host computer, is despatched by the software along what is perceived to be the most appropriate route, from network to network, until it reaches the required destination.

Client-server technology underlies much of the Internet. Server computers disseminate information resources, and these are retrieved by client machines on global or local computer networks. In other words, you run a client program on your workstation which opens connections to remote computers, requests data from them, and receives and displays the resulting information. The server software runs on the remote computer you access, and can normally handle information requests from many clients simultaneously.

No single organization or individual controls the Internet, and for this reason it is often described as anarchic. Nevertheless, there are key individuals and groups who monitor the Internet and who have influenced its development. The World Wide Web Consortium (W3C) was founded in October 1994 to realize the potential of the world wide web by 'developing common protocols that promote its evolution and ensure its interoperability'. Services provided by the Consortium include: reference information about the world wide web for developers and users; reference code implementations to embody and promote standards; and various prototype and sample applications to demonstrate use of new technology. Membership of W3C is open to any organization that signs a membership agreement. Its Internet address or URL (explained in Chapter 2) is:

http://www.w3.org/Consortium/

Other organizations which play a role in influencing the way the Internet develops include:

The Internet Society (ISOC)
http://www.isoc.org/
which is a non-governmental international organization for global cooperation and coordination for the Internet and its Internet-working technologies and applications;

The Internet Engineering Task Force (IETF)
http://www.ietf.org/
which is the principal body engaged in the development of new Internet standard specifications; and

The Internet Watch Foundation (IWF)
http://www.iwf.org.uk/
which was launched in 1996 to address the problem of illegal material on the Internet, with particular reference to child pornography. It is an independent organization formed to implement the proposals jointly agreed by the government, the police and the two major UK Internet Service Provider trade associations.

The Internet was originally used by education and military researchers, but the recent huge growth in commercial use means that other organizations now exert a major influence. Computer and communications companies like Microsoft and Netscape market Internet products such as browsers (see Chapter 6) that by their widespread use set standards that others have to meet to compete.

One source which provides valuable background information about the Internet and its applications is *LivingInternet.com*:

http://www.livinginternet.com/

Access to the Internet

Access to the Internet is provided by Internet Service Providers (ISPs). Selection of an ISP for a public library will normally be made at authority level, but you may wish to set up access at home or be asked to advise others. Since 1998, a growing number of ISPs have offered free access to the Internet, requiring only telecommunications costs to be found. During the early months of 2000, a number of companies announced free and low-tariff telecoms charges for Internet access. Selecting from the wide range of ISPs and telecommunications carriers is now a very complex choice.

Be careful not to commit yourself to one Internet Service Provider for too long a period initially, as you may well wish to change ISP as your knowledge increases and your requirements change.

For the latest comparative information about Internet Service Providers, it is advisable to consult the monthly magazines about the Internet that are published in the UK (see Chapter 14).

Listings of Internet Service Providers in the UK include:

The list
http://thelist.internet.com/countrycode/44.html

Internet access providers in UK & Ireland (InternetUK)
http://www.limitless.co.uk/inetuk/providers.html

Comparative information about the facilities offered by free ISPs is available from the *net4nowt* website:
http://www.net4nowt.com/

Other listings of free ISPs include:

Free Internet Access in UK & Ireland (InternetUK)
http://www.limitless.co.uk/inetuk/free-access.html

Free ISP Index (Easy as 1-2-Free)
http://www.12free.co.uk/ispidx.htm

Individuals without access to the Internet through their place of work or study can access the Internet in cybercafés and of course in a growing number of public libraries.

The EARL website provides a listing of UK public libraries offering Internet access (this can be browsed by town or local authority):

http://www.earl.org.uk/access/index.html

Listings of UK cybercafés are available from:

UK Index
http://www.ukindex.co.uk/cybercfe.html

Internet Magazine
http://www.internet-magazine.com/resource/cybercafes/index.html

Alternatively, run a search on 'cyber cafe' in *Yahoo! UK and Ireland*:

http://uk.yahoo.com/

Internet Service Providers will normally provide guidance on what constitutes *acceptable use* of their service, which you will need to pass on to users. This relates in part to resourcing (eg users are likely to be allocated a finite amount of file storage space) and in part to the use made of the service. In the public sector, the parents or guardians of minors must be warned about the range of resources available on the Internet. Library services will inevitably at some point have to decide on the extent to which they can block access to pornography and other potentially offensive material. Acceptable use and other issues related to public library service provision are discussed in greater detail in Chapter 24.

Chapter 3 discusses some aspects of netiquette (or network etiquette) as it relates to e-mail communication. Filtering is the term used to describe the use of software which restricts access to certain categories of material on the Internet; such software is usually designed to try to prevent access to pornography and other potentially offensive material. The EARL Networked Services Policy Taskgroup has produced a document on the issue of filtering:

http://www.earl.org.uk/taskgroups/policy/issue_papers/filtering.htm

Information on filtering issues and software from a US viewpoint is available at:

http://www.librarylandindex.org/cen/cens.htm

There is an increasing concern about the 'accessibility' of the Internet for users with disabilities. A useful collection of resources for the visually impaired is available through *NetLearn*:

http://www.rgu.ac.uk/~sim/research/netlearn/visually.htm

We return to these issues in Chapter 22 which deals with the production of web pages.

Statistics and demographics

It is claimed that statistics can be made to prove anything and statistics concerning Internet size and usage are less precise than most, often relying mainly on estimates. Nevertheless, one valuable site for demographic and other Internet surveys is provided by Nua, an Internet consultancy and developer which specializes in projects for large organizations and software companies:

NUA Internet surveys
http://www.nua.ie/surveys/
include business, social, technical and demographic surveys.

How many online?
http://www.nua.ie/surveys/how_many_online/index.html
provides an 'educated guess' as to how many people are online worldwide in the current month. In March 2000 this was 304.36 million.

CyberAtlas
http://www.cyberatlas.com/
also provides a selection of Internet demographics and statistics, particularly focusing on market size and usage patterns.
Yahoo! also includes links to a variety of services that provide these statistics:
http://uk.dir.yahoo.com/Computers_and_Internet/Internet/Statistics_and_Demographics/

What you will and won't find on the Internet

This book discusses different information resources found on the Internet. The types of resources available include:

- ★ text: reports, articles, books, newspapers, directories and databases
- ★ images: graphics, photographs and video clips
- ★ sound: speeches, music and real-time radio
- ★ software: freeware, shareware, evaluation copies and upgrades of commercial products
- ★ junk!

Internet resources complement library stock. In some cases the Internet can be used to update or supplement information found in standard reference works, or to provide the context or background detail to a query that will enable the answer to be located. New web-based subscription resources, such as *KnowUK* may well replace standard printed reference works in the library:

http://www.knowuk.co.uk/

A useful document, *Internet services: the range available to library users* (produced by the EARL Networked Services Policy Taskgroup), is available at:

http://www.earl.org.uk/taskgroups/policy/issue_papers/range.htm

The Internet has proved to be particularly invaluable in relation to information that will not be static for long enough to be published in printed form (such as the list of cybercafés mentioned previously) or that needs to be updated regularly (such as product directories or sports results).

The Internet is also used for distributing information that is ephemeral or of little long-term commercial value (eg family history). Individuals with the time and interest to collect information on their hobbies or leisure interests have found the Internet an ideal medium through which to provide newsletters, fanzines, facts and figures, and even software. However, enthusiasm and circumstances can change, so these websites can be short-lived. Topics that have a high profile in the media and the professional press tend to be prominent on the Internet as well. Major growth areas for information websites include travel, entertainment, food, health and pharmaceutical information, financial and other consumer information, electronic news, school league tables, paintings, dictionaries, statistics, maps and job vacancies.

However, information that costs a lot to create and/or collect (such as company financial data), or that is primarily of commercial value, is unlikely to be available free of charge on the Internet – but the Internet is an important way of delivering such paid-for services. What you will be able to retrieve without charge includes software, background information on companies, product information, the text of out-of-copyright books, and web pages from a wide range of providers including the Government, education, voluntary organizations and self-help groups. The Internet is also used to distribute resources found in another medium – such as the wide range of online versions of newspapers and magazines (see Chapter 18).

Selling services and goods over the Internet (e-commerce) is a major growth area. In addition to the Internet-only companies, all major corporations now have an Internet presence although some high street names have still to set up their sites for full electronic trading. Although many individuals are still hesitant to shop via the Internet, they may well use the Internet to source goods and services before purchasing through more conventional means.

Ultimately, any information that you find on the Internet will only be as good as the provider makes it. It is important to be critical in relation to resources distributed via the Internet, whether these are web pages, databases, software, or discussion list or Usenet messages. You need to consider whether these are accurate, comprehensive and up-to-date – the best web pages, for example, will provide information about the individual or organization that authored them as well as the date on which they were last updated. In addition, learning to distinguish between facts and opinions is vital. Fortunately, there are a number of websites which provide guidance in evaluating Internet resources; such as the BBC's *WebWise guide to quality information research on the Internet* [**http://www.bbc.co.uk/webwise/know/quality_1.shtml**], the *Internet Detective* tutorial [**http://sosig.ac.uk/desire/internet-detective.html**] and the *World-Wide Web Virtual Library*'s listing of evaluation resources [**http://www.vuw.ac.nz/~agsmith/evaln/evaln.htm**].

2

Understanding and using Internet addresses

- ★ How addresses are constructed
- ★ Why you need to know
- ★ Finding addresses

How addresses are constructed

Since the Internet comprises huge numbers of computers, and involves communication between them, there clearly needs to be a way of identifying each machine and this is done by means of an address. Each computer connected to the Internet has a unique address (similar to a postal address or a phone number) to allow users to contact it, whether for e-mail, to call up information or to use some software. This may sometimes be the same as the URL (Uniform Resource Locator) for a web page, but not always, as the URL can point to particular files on a machine. This Internet Protocol, or IP, address is made up of four sets of digits, eg 192.112.36.5. Your machine may have its own address or more likely you will connect to the Internet through one – a library server or an Internet Service Provider – that does. Though computers use these addresses it is difficult for people to remember them, so a variant system using names has become universal – you will rarely see an address in the numerical format.These two forms of address are linked in an international database called the Domain Name System (DNS) and follow prescribed patterns.

All addresses have at least two parts – an organization name, and the domain or type of organization – but may have three, four or five parts. A typical address is that for the library catalogue at the University of Northumbria at Newcastle:

opac.unn.ac.uk

The parts of the address represent the name of a particular **computer** – **opac** – at a particular **organization** – the University of Northumbria, here abbreviated to **unn** – in the **academic** domain – **ac** – and in a particular **country** – the UK. The address is pronounced opac dot unn dot ac dot uk. Addresses are usually by convention printed in lower-case letters, though they could be written in upper case – it does not matter.

Other computers at Northumbria have addresses such as **hswe.unn.ac.uk** or **personnel.unn.ac.uk.**

Non-academic organizations have other codes for their domain and often don't have a computer name, eg:

waterstones.co.uk
a company

la-hq.org.uk
a non-profit organization: The Library Association

coi.gov.uk
a government body: the Central Office of Information.

Other countries' addresses have the internationally agreed country code and may not have a domain, eg:

springer.de
Germany

nissan.co.jp
Japan

These can occasionally be used in other ways, such as the GCSE revision site **http://www.revise.it**, which is based in the UK and not Italy.

The exception to this format is the USA, where you will rarely see the **us** code used. This is because they invented the Internet, just as British postage stamps have no country name because we invented them!

Instead US addresses have three-character domain names:

whitehouse.gov
government

dialog.com
a company

www.ala.org
a non-profit organization

ceth.rutgers.edu
an educational establishment

rs.internic.net
a network administrative body

www.dac.army.mil
a military organization.

However, many non US-based organizations now also use the **.com** domain, for example:

www.the-stationery-office.com
heineken.com

This is usually to give themselves a more international image or to reflect the international nature of their activities and is seen as particularly necessary for anyone involved in e-commerce.

Some international organizations have an **int** code, eg:

europa.eu.int

We are also beginning to see variations such as **uk.com**. For some time there have been pressures to allow more domains, so as to reflect more fully the range of organizations using the Internet and get away from what some see as restrictions arising from the Internet's military and academic origins. Some new domains proposed include **.shop**, **.firm**, **.arts**, **.football.uk** and **.per.uk** (for personal sites).

Using addresses

You will need to use addresses when sending electronic mail (see Chapter 3) and when connecting to various remote resources using telnet or on the world wide web (see Chapter 4). However, you will not always need to key them in: in many cases you will just follow hyperlinks in web pages or you will build up your own collection of those you find most useful in a 'bookmark' or 'favorites' list, and often for e-mail addresses you can just copy and paste them from some source.

Nevertheless, it is always useful to know how addresses are put together. Sometimes there may be an error in an address, or you may not know the address of some particular organization you want to contact but can make a good guess what it might be. So a www (world wide web) machine frequently has an address in the form *www.organization.domain.country*, eg:

www.ox.ac.uk

www.amazon.co.uk

and commercial companies like to include an obvious version of their name, eg: **www.the-body-shop.com** (though you might guess this one as **www.bodyshop.co.uk** or some other variant!).

Finding addresses

There is no overall list of Internet addresses to consult, but there are various ways of finding them.

If you need an address for electronic mail then some sources are discussed in Chapter 3. If you want a web or telnet address for a particular organization, and guessing the likely form of the address does not work, then you can try a subject collection like *Excite* or *Yahoo!* (discussed in Chapter 5) or one of the world wide web search services like *AltaVista* or *Northern Light*, also discussed in Chapter 5. The latter services index millions of pages of information on the Internet, so will usually find those from any organization you specify and show the address. In some cases the search can be limited to words in the address only, and not in the text of pages, so simplifying the process.

3

Essential communication skills on the Internet

- ★ Using electronic mail to communicate with individuals
  - – Viruses
  - – Spamming
- ★ Using discussion lists and newsgroups to share information and experience on a subject
- ★ Network etiquette – good practice in using mail

Electronic mail

The first use of the Internet for most people is to communicate with other users – and there are millions of them worldwide – using electronic mail.

Electronic mail, or e-mail, is a means of sending a message – from a few lines to many pages – from your computer, or more likely from the space allocated to you on your service provider's system, to someone else's space elsewhere. This person's space may be in your own library or anywhere on the Internet. The process is generally quick – a few seconds to reach someone in your own institution; minutes, maybe hours, to the other side of the world. (On a bad day it can take hours for short distances!)

You simply type in your message and the address to which it is to be sent, and send the message. The recipient has to check his/her 'mailbox' to see what messages have been received. It's a bit like a telephone answering machine and has the same advantage that you can send the message without the other person being there. Even more usefully you can send the same message to many people just as easily as to one.

Uses might be for general communication within your library or authority or to contact suppliers, information providers and so on, or to contribute to a discussion list (see below). You might wish to offer e-mail as a service for your users. More interestingly, your library might provide a public enquiry service based on e-mail, though if you do, make clear to users what sort of turnaround time to expect: e-mail has an immediacy that raises expectations of instant replies! An example of such a service is that from libraries in the North East of England at **http://www.thenortheast.com/ask.html**.

E-mail software

There are many different types of e-mail software, such as Pine, Elm, Eudora, Pegasus and Microsoft Outlook. Your organization may have a standard one or it may depend on the Internet Service Provider you use. Most have a Windows environment with menus to choose options from; older software will require you to enter commands. Clearly, because of this variety, detailed procedures cannot be given here, but all mail systems should allow you to:

- ★ edit a message offline before you send it
- ★ cut and paste text/addresses from and to messages
- ★ reply to a message received, quoting text from the original if desired
- ★ forward a message you have received to someone else
- ★ store messages for future reference, if necessary in folders or directories
- ★ print messages
- ★ delete messages
- ★ create a mailing list to send a message to a group of people
- ★ send a file of text already created
- ★ save a message you have received as a file so that you can edit it
- ★ consult an address book of mail addresses
- ★ set up an 'alias' – a short form of address – for frequently used addresses, so you can type 'bill' instead of 'bill.oswaldtwistle@library.westyorkshire.gov.uk'

If you are connecting to the Internet through a commercial service, then, to save phone charges, your mail system might allow messages to be downloaded and then read offline.

Figure 3.1 shows a typical message with a lot of information at the beginning (the header) relating to the route the message has taken. This may not always be present, or may be hidden by the software and is mostly not important. Your mail address is normally added automatically but you should include it and your name and, if appropriate, your library and mail address at

Delivered-To: freemail.net-jane.brown@lamail.net
Return-Path: <newsletter@mtn.co.uk>
X-Envelope-To: jane.brown@lamail.net
X-Envelope-From: newsletter@mtn.co.uk
X-Delivery-Time: 949606057
Received: (qmail 22271 invoked from network); 3 Feb 2000 19:27:37 -0000
Received: from firestorm.mail.pipex.net (158.43.128.80)
 by icestorm.mail.pipex.net with SMTP; 3 Feb 2000 19:27:37 -0000
Received: (qmail 8215 invoked from network); 3 Feb 2000 19:26:44 -0000
Received: from mail1-gui.server.which.net (194.168.97.3)
 by depot.dial.pipex.com with SMTP; 3 Feb 2000 19:26:44 -0000
Received: from localhost ([194.168.100.24]) by mail1-gui.server.which.net
 (Post.Office MTA v3.1.2 release (PO203-101c)
 ID# 0-33929U70000L2S50) with SMTP id AAU233
 for <jane.brown@lamail.net>; Thu, 3 Feb 2000 19:27:27 +0000
From: editor <newsletter@mtn.co.uk>
To: Jane Brown <jane.brown@lamail.net>
Date: Thu, 03 Feb 2000 19:19:51 +0000
Subject: MtN Newsletter: All Change
Reply-To: newsletter@mtn.co.uk
Organization: MtN Sports
MIME-Version: 1.0
Content-Type: text/plain; charset=us-ascii
Content-Transfer-Encoding: 7bit
X-Priority: 3

MtN Sports Newsletter
"UK Mountain Sports - Online"
http://www.mtn.co.uk

Hello Jane
During February, MtN is being split into two. MtN will concentrate on hillwalking, trekking and backpacking. A new site, ClimbUK, will cater for climbers at http://www.climbuk.com and http://www.climbing.co.uk

Nordic skiing will continue on MtN, until our Nordic site is up and running in March.

We hope you have the opportunity to look at ClimbUK and we welcome any positive criticism, suggestions and bug reports.

Best wishes
David Button
Editor, MtN Sports
http://www.mtn.co.uk

Fig. 3.1 *The 'header' information in an e-mail*

the end of your message. Some people use a signature file giving more information such as phone and fax numbers, or even a witty quote, which can be added automatically or easily to your message. (If you use a quote change it frequently – the wittiness soon palls!)

Mail messages are usually simple text files, though some can also create messages in HTML (the web page language) or RTF (Rich Text Format) that allow a variety of fonts or other ways of emphasizing text. However, since many mail systems cannot read these formats and would show the message as plain text there's no great advantage in using them. Most mail systems will also allow you to send more complex files, such as a word-processed document, a spreadsheet or an image, as an 'attachment' to your message. However, these can be very large files so, if you send an attachment, you need to be sure that your recipient's system can deal with it and that they have enough filespace for it. Many discussion lists discourage the use of attachments.

Some good practice

- ★ You should always put a useful title in the **Subject**: line. Many people get lots of messages a day (perhaps 100 or more) and will scan their list of messages to see which to read first – and maybe delete uninteresting-looking ones without reading them.
- ★ The use of shorthand convention in messages is sometimes encouraged to save time – eg BTW for by the way, IMHO for in my humble opinion – but these should be used sparingly.
- ★ Similarly there can be the use of 'smileys' or 'emoticons' to add more meaning to messages, such as :-) for happy. There are large numbers of these, but their meaning is never very obvious and they are best ignored.
- ★ You need to manage your messages since you may have limited space for storing them. You should get into the habit of checking your message files regularly and deleting those you no longer need. It can be easy to acquire a few hundred messages, particularly if you are on discussion lists.
- ★ Don't use long lines in a message as they will probably wrap round in other people's mail programs – around 70 characters is appropriate. Your mail program should allow you to set this length.
- ★ Plain text messages cannot include a pound sign so always spell out the word.

Free e-mail

As well as e-mail provided at work you will have an alternative if you have Internet access at home, but it is also possible to have free web-based mail from services like *Excite*, *Hotmail* and *Freeserve*.

See a list at:

http://www.emailaddresses.com/

These services have the advantage that you can use them from anywhere with a web browser, rather than having to log on to a particular computer system, but they are free because you have to endure advertising and the service may be poor, partly because all messages, even to someone in the same room, have to go via the web mail-server which might be in the USA. They will not have the same facilities as a full e-mail service.

If you wish to offer an e-mail service for your users then these are an alternative to that from your Internet Service Provider. On the other hand, if you do not offer a service you will find users bypassing this restriction by using a web-based service. If this is not acceptable you may need to monitor what they are doing. Free e-mail services are also discussed in Chapter 14.

Viruses

You are probably aware of computer viruses that can, at worst, destroy all the work on your computer and, at best, just be a nuisance. People worry that these can be passed on by e-mail and you may see messages warning you not to read a message with a particular heading because it contains a deadly virus. Be reassured that an e-mail message cannot normally contain a virus. See:

Computer virus myths

http://www.kumite.com/myths/home.htm

Internet hoaxes

http://ciac.llnl.gov/ciac/CIACHoaxes.html

which give details of common hoax viruses.

However, if the message has an *attachment*, such as a word-processed document, then this could have a species known as a 'macro virus', though it is unlikely. Nevertheless you should make sure your system, or your own PC, has anti-virus software, such as McAfee Virus Scan or Norton Anti-Virus, that will warn you of viruses and allow you to deal with them. It is important to upgrade this software regularly – preferably weekly. As a further precaution you should not open attachments or any files ending in .exe (known as executable files) from sources whose validity you are unsure of, though even this principle is not always helpful, as some of the latest macro viruses arrive in a message purporting to come from someone you know.

Spamming

Just as there are junk mail and junk faxes, so there is junk e-mail, or 'spam' as it is often known. Spammers acquire mailing lists and send their advertising to thousands of mail addresses. Messages may sometimes be for legitimate products, but mostly are inviting you to participate in some get-rich-quick scheme or to visit a particularly hot adult website. Spam is usually obvious from the mail header and you can simply delete it without reading. If you want to prevent it reaching you then you can use filtering software that may be part of your mail system or that you can obtain, probably for nothing. This checks incoming mail for specified words and refuses any containing them. It can also be used for coping with your normal mail, but this sort of filtering is not especially effective and can exclude messages you want to see.

For more information see: *Coalition Against Unsolicited Commercial Email* **http://www.spam.abuse.net**

E-mail addresses

In Chapter 2 we showed how the address for a particular computer is formed. An e-mail address simply adds the identity of the person concerned in the form **person@place**. (Note that @ is pronounced 'at'.) This identity may be a string of characters like **vhf45**, which could be your ID to log on to your local system, or it may be a more meaningful real name. The place may be just the organization name or may be a particular machine.

Examples:

vhf45@library.gold.ac.uk
marygreen@aol.com
j.charlton@leedsutd.freeserve.co.uk

Finding addresses

E-mail addresses are allocated by the institution/service provider concerned and there are no comprehensive national directories as there are for telephone numbers. Finding someone's address may be tricky, and not always possible, but there are a number of places to try. You can usually search on first and last names, and maybe a place or organization too. The lists vary in their accuracy and may include out-of-date addresses. Many are concerned mainly with US addresses and are poor for the UK. There is no best one – just try them all.

People Search – Yahoo's e-mail directory
http://ukie.people.yahoo.com/

Internet Address Finder
http://www.iaf.net

Bigfoot
http://www.bigfoot.com/

Infospace.com
http://www.infospace.com/

MESA – Meta Email Search Agent
http://mesa.rrzn.uni-hannover.de

Switchboard.com
http://www.switchboard.com/

Whowhere
http://www.whowhere.com/

Your Internet Service Provider may have other directories or indeed may use some of these.

The Mailbase service (discussed below) can be used to find the addresses of people who have subscribed to their discussion lists. These will mostly be in the UK.

Mailbase
http://www.mailbase.ac.uk/

If you know the institution someone belongs to you may be able to find details on its web service. (See Chapter 4 for some lists of web services.)

Discussion lists

A discussion list uses e-mail to create a worldwide forum to:

★ discuss topics
★ ask and answer questions
★ pass on news – eg meetings, job vacancies, professional developments
★ share information on a particular subject

and so on.

A similar function is provided by Usenet newsgroups (see below), with each list or newsgroup dealing with a particular topic area.

Lists tend to cover academic subjects more than newsgroups do, though there are also many for recreational topics. Subjects are as varied as British fiction, Rudyard Kipling or military history. A list will be based in one country – most are in the USA – but open for anyone anywhere to join, though the membership and content may reflect that country.

You are probably only likely to join lists dealing with professional activity, but you may want to direct users to other lists or to search message archives (see Chapter 5).

Joining a list

If you choose to join a list you do so by sending an e-mail message to register.

The message will be something like

```
subscribe listname Bill Brown
```

(if your name is Bill Brown). You do not need to include your e-mail address as that is extracted automatically from your message.

You send this message to an administrative address which has the form:

```
listserv@thvm.cmu.edu
majordomo@thvm.cmu.edu
```

for most US-based lists, or:

```
mailbase@mailbase.ac.uk
```

for those on Mailbase.

Registration is done automatically by a program and you will receive confirmation and instructions on how to use the list, notification of whether there is an archive of past messages and so on. Some lists offer the opportunity to receive messages in digest form – that is, you do not receive them individually, but in batches, usually at particular intervals.

The Mailbase website noted above includes details of their procedures, and a user guide for lists using the Listserv program is at:

http://www.lsoft.com/manuals/userindex.html

However, there is always a person – the list owner – whom you can contact if you have problems.

Messages are sent to the list address – and normally are automatically distributed to all those who are registered on the list. Note: the list address is in the form

listname@somewhere

such as **lis-link@mailbase.ac.uk** – and is not the same as the administrative address shown above. Inevitably you will send something to the list instead of the administrative address, but don't worry – we've all made that mistake! Some lists are 'moderated', ie messages are processed by a person – usually to give some coordination, but occasionally to control what is being sent.

There is no obligation to contribute to a list, and you will probably benefit just from listening in to the discussion ('lurking') or reading news items.

Some hints on good practice in using lists can be found later in this chapter. You can also see some general background information at *Mary Houten-Kemp's everything e-mail*:

http://everythingemail.net

Finding what lists there are

There are tens of thousands of lists out there, and a number of directories exist to help you discover them. These always include instructions on how to join a particular list. Despite the large numbers, lists do not exist for every subject you might want.

'Serious' lists in the UK are mostly part of the Mailbase project developed at Newcastle University. Originally restricted to UK higher education, these now have an international membership. There is a central service:

http://www.mailbase.ac.uk/

that lists all the lists and for each gives a description, a directory of all the members, and a two-year archive of messages that have been sent to the list. (Figure 3.2 shows a section from a list of messages on the *lis-pub-libs* list.) You can search list names and descriptions by subject or browse by subject groups,

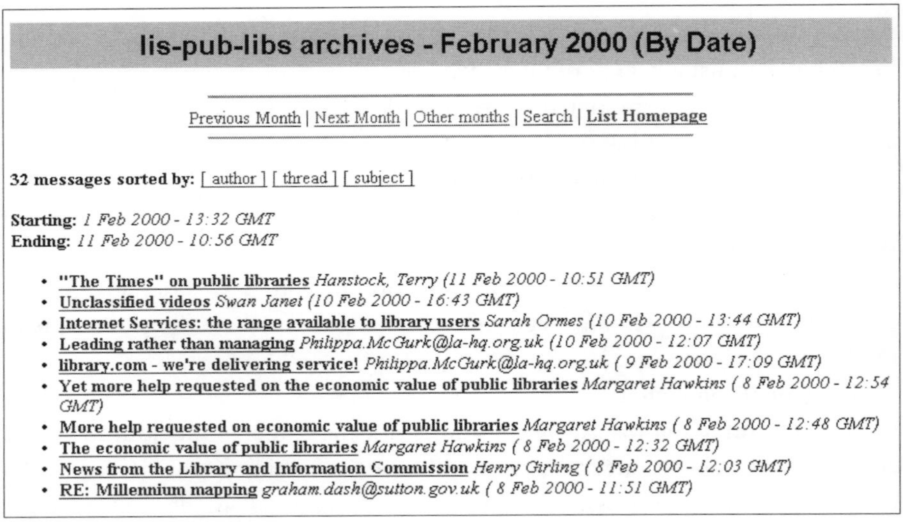

lis-pub-libs archives - February 2000 (By Date)

Previous Month | Next Month | Other months | Search | **List Homepage**

32 messages sorted by: [author] [thread] [subject]

Starting: *1 Feb 2000 - 13:32 GMT*
Ending: *11 Feb 2000 - 10:56 GMT*

- **"The Times" on public libraries** *Hanstock, Terry (11 Feb 2000 - 10:51 GMT)*
- **Unclassified videos** *Swan Janet (10 Feb 2000 - 16:43 GMT)*
- **Internet Services: the range available to library users** *Sarah Ormes (10 Feb 2000 - 13:44 GMT)*
- **Leading rather than managing** *Philippa.McGurk@la-hq.org.uk (10 Feb 2000 - 12:07 GMT)*
- **library.com - we're delivering service!** *Philippa.McGurk@la-hq.org.uk (9 Feb 2000 - 17:09 GMT)*
- **Yet more help requested on the economic value of public libraries** *Margaret Hawkins (8 Feb 2000 - 12:54 GMT)*
- **More help requested on economic value of public libraries** *Margaret Hawkins (8 Feb 2000 - 12:48 GMT)*
- **The economic value of public libraries** *Margaret Hawkins (8 Feb 2000 - 12:32 GMT)*
- **News from the Library and Information Commission** *Henry Girling (8 Feb 2000 - 12:03 GMT)*
- **RE: Millennium mapping** *graham.dash@sutton.gov.uk (8 Feb 2000 - 11:51 GMT)*

Fig. 3.2 *List of messages from the* lis-pub-libs *list*

such as public libraries and official publications. If you find a list that looks relevant, you can check the message archive to see what sort of topics are discussed before deciding whether to join.

There are lists for many aspects of LIS activity such as *lis-ill*, *lis-law*, *lis-maps* and *lis-serials*.

There is also the general *lis-link* list to which at least one person from each library should belong.

Other directories have a worldwide coverage but unlike the Mailbase site do not include lists of members or message archives.

Directory of Scholarly Electronic Conferences
http://www.n2h2.com/KOVACS
concentrates on scholarly lists worldwide. Only a brief description is included. You can search list names and descriptions or browse the lists for a subject area.

For a directory of all types of list, including the Usenet newsgroups described below, try:

Liszt
http://www.liszt.com/
which has over 90,000 lists indexed or:

Tile.Net
http://tile.net/lists

To find library-related lists you can consult:

Library oriented lists and electronic serials
http://www.wrlc.org/Liblists

which will give you details of, for example, *SPIN-L*, the SilverPlatter list, and *Stumpers-L* for reference questions, but has only selected Mailbase lists.

Usenet newsgroups

Usenet is one of the oldest uses of the Internet, being created in 1979 by students in North America who wished to link together people who shared common interests. Today it is a conferencing system in which any user can participate in the discussion of a wide range of topics covered by over 30,000 newsgroups. Each newsgroup contains articles or messages which may be grouped in 'threads' or themes. They have a similar function to discussion lists, and users can post (send) and reply to messages, mail interesting articles to themselves and usually access archives. As with lists, some newsgroups are moderated. The range of subjects is immense, ranging from very technical computing topics to the weird, the trivial and the downright obscene. This is the place to find the crazy people on the Net!

Usenet is in essence a huge, continuously updated database that users must consult to read messages – they do not arrive in a mailbox. It requires a very large amount of storage space so messages may not be available for more than a few days and, indeed, your service provider may offer only a selection of newsgroups and possibly none at all. You can look at any of the newsgroups, but will normally subscribe to (select) those you want to see regularly – for convenience only these will be displayed when you connect.

Newsgroup names are organized in hierarchies with a number of categories, including:

alt 'alternative' discussions
biz business
bionet biological sciences
comp computer hardware and software, computer science
news news about Usenet
rec hobbies and leisure interests
sci research in the sciences
soc social issues and world cultures
uk newsgroups specifically on UK topics

Here you will find the *alt.support* series for various illnesses, professional groups like *misc.health.therapy.occupational*, issues newsgroups such as *uk.politics.drugs*, fan groups such as *uk.media.tv.friends* and the silly ones like *alt.2eggs.sausage.beans.2tomatoes.2toast.largetea.cheerslove!*

There are few in the LIS area. Newsgroups are less used by academics and professionals than discussion lists, but can be valuable for getting help with practical problems. You may want to use them yourself or to let users post messages.

Accessing newsgroups

To access newsgroups you will require software known as a newsreader. In some cases this may be a text-based reader (such as Tin or Pine), but more likely a newsreading facility will be included in your web browser or e-mail system. An alternative is to download Free Agent from:

http://www.forteinc.com/getfa/getfa.htm

This is a useful offline newsreader that you use to download messages, then disconnect and read them, so saving telephone costs.

Figure 3.3 shows a typical list of messages on the *uk.transport* newsgroup using Microsoft Outlook Express.

uk.transport — Main Identity

Subject	From	Sent	Size
Looking for	steve	06/03/00 01:12	1KB
Lorry over Barton Bridge	crumble	06/03/00 04:23	1KB
Re: Holing out (was Re: Council neglig...	David Wheeler	06/03/00 08:26	2KB
30 mph limit a failure.	John Wright	06/03/00 09:33	2KB
Re: Reducing accidents - a rant	Matthew Black	06/03/00 09:39	1KB
Re: Short questionnaire pls participate	Gary Knighton	06/03/00 12:01	1KB
Re: Gatso - health hazard?	Andy Turner	06/03/00 12:12	2KB
Re: Prescott is a liar !!	Andy Turner	06/03/00 12:22	1KB
Re: Prescott is a liar !!	Andy Turner	06/03/00 12:47	4KB
Re: Prescott is a liar !!	Huge	06/03/00 13:12	2KB
Re: Prescott is a liar !!	Gary Jones	06/03/00 13:24	2KB
Re: Prescott is a liar !!	Robin Payne	06/03/00 13:54	2KB
Re: Prescott is a liar !!	Dave Hillam	06/03/00 22:39	1KB
Re: Prescott is a liar !!	Andy Turner	07/03/00 01:07	1KB
Turning hard shoulder into extra motorw...	Steve Pearce	06/03/00 13:29	1KB
Website Update 6 March 2000	Ship Technology	06/03/00 14:44	4KB
Tokens and transport systems	Paul Baker	06/03/00 20:39	1KB
Signalling systems (was: Prescott is a li...	Aidan Stanger	06/03/00 22:22	4KB
Re: Anti-Speed Protestors "Misguided"...	John Wright	07/03/00 09:22	2KB
Re: Thameslink rant	Spencer Lane	07/03/00 12:16	1KB
New type of speed camera	Martin Fiddler	07/03/00 15:49	2KB
Re: New type of speed camera	John Burns	07/03/00 18:43	2KB

300 message(s), 300 unread, 2257 not downloaded — Working Online

Fig. 3.3 *Typical list of messages on the* uk.transport *newsgroup*

Identifying newsgroups of potential interest can be done in a variety of ways – you can simply browse down the hierarchies accessible to you, or consult a listing such as *Tile.Net* (see above).

If you do not have Usenet access as part of your Internet service you can read and post messages on web-based services at:

Deja.com
http://www.deja.com/usenet

RemarQ
http://www.remarq.com/

Searching message archives is covered in Chapter 5.

Details of UK newsgroups can be found on the *UK Usenet home pages*:
http://www.usenet.org.uk/

A more general source of background information for new users can be found in the *news.announce.newusers* newsgroup. This newsgroup normally includes regular postings of articles entitled 'What is Usenet?' and 'Frequently asked questions about Usenet'.

The latter is an example of a FAQ or Frequently Asked Question. FAQs are files of information on a topic covered by a newsgroup. Since newsgroups range in subject from the erudite to the exotic, FAQs can deal with topics such as epilepsy, UK transport or a guide to vegetarian restaurants in Europe. Some may be excellent introductions to their subject. Each FAQ is distributed on one or more relevant newsgroups and should be updated and reissued regularly. There are collections of them, such as :

http://faqs.org/

You can browse by category or newsgroup or search the whole collection.

Netiquette

Netiquette, or network etiquette, refers to generally accepted standards of good practice in using e-mail, discussion lists and newsgroups. There is a need for some discipline to ensure that lists work effectively and that time and computer usage is not wasted. Not all users, especially in Usenet groups, respect the need for this.

The following are some useful common guidelines. Your users should be made aware of these.

- ★ Remember that mail systems are not especially secure or necessarily private, so don't use e-mail for confidential or otherwise sensitive communication. Think of a mail message as being similar to a message written on a postcard. Remember also that messages can usually be traced back to the sender.
- ★ Lists and newsgroups are intended to be a civilized forum, and the bad temper, abuse or anger that might occur in a face-to-face discussion is not appreciated. (Such electronic anger is usually known as 'flaming'.) Remember that the law can be applied to electronic communication, so don't make comments about someone that could, for example, be libellous or racist.
- ★ Do not ask trivial questions on a list or newsgroup that could be answered more easily in other ways (eg by looking in a book). They are likely to be ignored.
- ★ Do not ask questions that would require someone to do research for you. Ask specific questions, if necessary telling people what you already know, and don't expect long or comprehensive answers. A response is more likely from someone if the question can draw on their experience.
- ★ Nevertheless, do not be inhibited by feeling ignorant or overawed by the presence of experienced users on lists – many others are beginners too. 'I'm new to this list so this may have been asked before' is often a useful introduction.
- ★ If you ask a question send a summary of the replies to the list/newsgroup after a week or so.
- ★ Be considerate to others and allow for their mistakes. Do not reprimand people for not understanding procedures properly.
- ★ Brief comments are more likely to be widely read and to generate replies.
- ★ Try to respond to queries if you have something to contribute – lack of response is disheartening.
- ★ Lists can be a useful place to distribute questionnaires, but keep them short and don't expect a huge response.
- ★ Do not send 'chain letters': they are an abuse of the system that can slow down mail for others.

If you want more extensive guidelines try *The Net: user guidelines and netiquette* by Arlene Rinaldi:

http://www.fau.edu/netiquette

4

Net techniques explained

* ★ URLs
* ★ The world wide web
  - Browsers
  - Bookmarks and Favorites
  - URL and bookmark managers
  - Web servers around the world
  - E-mail access
  - Caching
  - Common problems
* ★ Telnet
* ★ File transfer protocol

Uniform Resource Locators (URLs)

The URL (or Uniform Resource Locator) is one form of Internet address, and is used to connect to servers, sites or pages around the world. URLs are a standard method of naming or specifying any kind of information on the Internet. The client computer that you use only needs to know what protocol (a set of data-exchange rules that computer systems use to talk to each other over the network) to expect of the desired information, and it retrieves it by that protocol. The user or web author specifies the format and protocol by using an appropriate URL.

Note that URLs are case sensitive, so take care when copying them down. Web pages with a ~ (the tilde sign) in the URL are normally personal pages provided by an individual.

A URL will usually specify three things:

<method>://<address>/<pathname>
<method> is the general kind of protocol or method used to retrieve the document. This will be **http** for HTML documents on the www; **ftp** for FTP; **news** for Usenet newsgroups; and **telnet** for telnet sessions. The method **file** can be used to refer to local files.

<address> refers to the computer (server) where the information or documents are stored. HTML and FTP documents all have a server on a specific host computer. Telnet sessions have a specific destination computer. Newsgroups are the only exception – instead of a host name, you provide a newsgroup (for example, **news:news.answers**). Newsgroups were described in the previous chapter, and telnet and FTP are explained later in this chapter.

<pathname> refers to the directory or file where the information is to be found. A URL for a directory usually ends with a / and that for a file with .htm or .html

Not all browsers require the **http://** prefix if the URL is for a website, and it is increasingly common for people to quote URLs without it as the majority of URLs that individuals deal with will be for websites. Browsers (see below) increasingly will 'fill in the blanks' if part of the Internet address is missing, eg typing 'ibm' into the **Location** box in later versions of Netscape Navigator will take the user to the IBM website at www.ibm.com; the Internet Explorer 'Autosearch' facility acts similarly.

Here are some sample URLs and explanations:

http://www.earl.org.uk/earlweb/index.html
An HTML document – the index page for the EARLweb reference tool for key information resources on the Internet.

ftp://rtfm.mit.edu/pub/usenet-by-group/news.answers/ftp-list/faq
An FTP file (actually a FAQ) at a computer at the Massachussets Institute of Technology, in the sub-directory /pub/usenet-by-group/news.answers/ftp-list/.

telnet:// bcmsv.leeds.ac.uk
The telnet address for an English verse collection at Leeds University.

The world wide web

The world wide web (often abbreviated to www or simply the web) is a hypertext-based system for finding and accessing Internet resources; it is now the dominant way of using the Internet. It can provide access to a variety of Internet resources from the same interface, including FTP sites and Usenet newsgroups, in addition to websites.

The world wide web is a distributed (in that it is not based in any single location), multimedia (combining text, still and moving images and sound), and hypertext (containing links to other documents, allowing information to be retrieved in a nonsequential way) system. It is thus a unique medium for communication and for publishing.

In order to improve the speed of access to popular websites, a mirror site (an exact copy) may be available in several continents.

Documents for the www are written in HTML (HyperText Markup Language).

Browsers

To access the world wide web, you need browser software. Within a library authority, computer support staff may decide on which product is to be supported across the organization. Most organizations running Windows95, Windows98, Windows 2000 or Windows NT will run Microsoft's Internet Explorer. The mainstream alternative is Netscape Communicator/Navigator which is available for PC, Macintosh and Unix platforms.

However, a range of alternative browser software products is available. One useful product is the Lynx browser which provides access to text information only, and can therefore be used in conjunction with speech-synthesizing software or enhanced screens.

Although the multimedia dimension is one of the main features of the web, if the information on the site you wish to consult is text based you can choose to switch off the *images* (pictures or graphics) when surfing the web. This allows a browser like Netscape or Internet Explorer to operate in a similar way to Lynx. Unfortunately not all www sites are set up to allow viewing in text-only mode.

Browser features include the ability to:

★ copy (save) a file to disk – in text or HTML form
★ print a file; if it contains images the process will be slow, and you may need a colour printer for best results
★ search the text of the file currently displayed

★ cut and paste text to other applications within a Windows environment
★ open/go to a specific URL that you key or paste in
★ interrupt a slow or unsuccessful file transfer
★ mail files to yourself.

Figure 4.1 shows the toolbars (row of icons) on Netscape Navigator and Microsoft Internet Explorer.

The requirement of seamless access to a wide variety of file formats (for example, PDF documents for electronic journals), Internet services (eg Usenet news) and audio and video files puts pressure on browser software. One solution is the development of modular browsers which allow additional plug-in or helper software to be added. Typical examples of the use of plug-ins are to access video or sound clips.

Although you may not have permission to customize, upgrade or even choose the browser software that you have access to at work, it can be helpful to be aware of the options that exist. *BrowserWatch*:

http://browserwatch.internet.com/

is a website with extensive information about browsers and plug-ins. It includes a list of browsers, and it indicates which platforms each browser supports or plans to support.

See also the *CNET Topic Center on Browsers*:

http://home.cnet.com/internet/0-3773.html

This includes links to tips and tutorials for both Internet Explorer and Netscape.

A list of some FAQs (frequently asked questions – and answers) on web browsers can be found at:

http://www.boutell.com/openfaq/browsers/

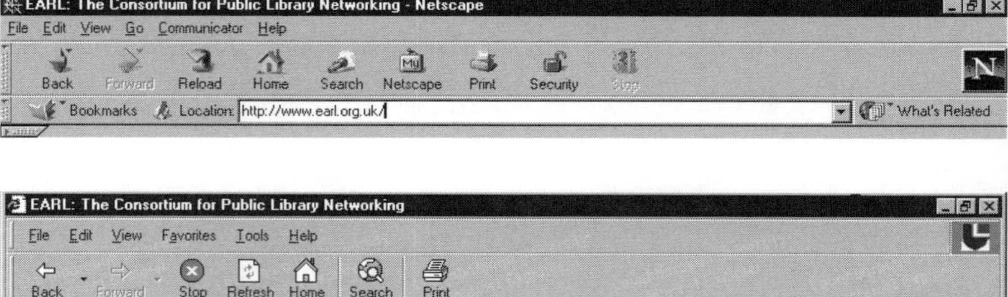

Fig. 4.1 *Toolbars from Netscape Navigator and Microsoft Explorer browsers*

Bookmarks and Favorites

A particularly important feature of browsers is the bookmark that records a document title and URL to enable you to revisit it when you wish to – just as a physical bookmark can take you to a particular page in a book. The bookmark feature on most browsers (called 'Favorites' in Internet Explorer) offers a short-cut back to a specific document. This is particularly useful when you find a document purely by chance while browsing the Internet, as it might otherwise be difficult to rediscover the site. You can save your bookmarks in order to pass them on to other people, or even use them as the basis for creating a web page.

In Netscape, to bookmark the document that you are presently viewing you choose the **Bookmarks** menu option and then **Add Bookmark**. Next time you click on the Bookmarks menu, the bookmark should appear in the list. To re-visit that site in future, all you need to do is click on the name of the document in the bookmark list. Similar facilities are offered within Internet Explorer using the **Favorites** menu.

Both Favorites and Bookmarks can be re-arranged into nested folders, which permits you to create a personal catalogue of useful Internet resources organized in a way that suits you. If you invest time developing and organizing your bookmarks, do back them up regularly.

Further information on organizing and using Bookmarks and Favorites can be found through the Help options for both Netscape and Internet Explorer. A number of tutorials are available including:

http://netforbeginners.about.com/internet/netforbeginners/library/weekly/aa110799.htm

A simple alternative to bookmarking sites (which is particularly useful if you are not using your own workstation at the time) is to mail the text of documents to yourself or to other people. In Netscape this can be done by using the **Send Page** command on the **File** menu; you may need to set up details of your e-mail address before you can mail a message (select **Preferences** from the **Edit** menu, then the **Mail & Newsgroups** menu and then select **Identity**). Using Internet Explorer, select **Mail & News** from the **Tools** menu, then choose **Send a Link**.

URL and bookmark managers

If you travel, move between machines, or keep losing bookmarks because you forget to back them up, one solution may be to use one of the growing number of URL and bookmark managers. These sites host your bookmarks/favorites on a web page with password access, after you have registered. Existing bookmarks/favorites can be imported.

Free bookmark managers include:

BookmarkBox
http://www.bookmarkbox.com/

BookmarksPlus
http://www.bookmarksplus.com/

Clickmarks
http://www.clickmarks.com/

ItList
http://www.itlist.com/

Murl
http://murl.com/

MyPassword.net
http://www.mypassword.net/

Other services are listed at:
http://www.davecentral.com/urlman.html

Web servers around the world

The number of websites is vast and growing rapidly and it is be impossible to list them all. None of the attempts to do so are complete, and you may need to use the search services described in Chapter 5 to trace the sites you want. However, collections or directories of web servers in particular subject areas or geographical regions can be of value.

Company sites

Company A–Z (Yell.com): alphabetical listing of commercial and business sites in the UK:
http://www.yell.co.uk/ukyw/atoz/index.html

UK index:
http://www.ukindex.co.uk/index.html

Government

Open.gov.uk: entry point to UK public sector information:
http://www.open.gov.uk/

Higher education

Universities Worldwide covers 147 countries and over 5000 institutions:
http://geowww.uibk.ac.at/univ/
An alternative source is *BRAINTRACK,* covering 152 countries:
http://www.braintrack.com/index.htm
Within the UK, the University of Wolverhampton *UK sensitive maps* of web servers covers universities, colleges and research sites:
http://www.scit.wlv.ac.uk/ukinfo/uk.map.html

Libraries

UK public libraries on the web (Sheila and Robert Harden):
http://dspace.dial.pipex.com/town/square/ac940/weblibs.html
Libraries online: links to collections of library websites (EARLweb):
http://www.earl.org.uk/earlweb/libs.html#Libraries

Schools

UK schools on the Internet:
http://schools.sys.uea.ac.uk/schools/schools.html

The voluntary sector

CharityNet aims to provide an international guide to non-profit data, links, sites and resources available on the web:
http://www.charitynet.org/
Charity Choice also provides an encyclopaedia of charities on the Internet:
http://www.charitychoice.co.uk/

E-mail access to the web

Occasionally you may only have limited access to the Internet because of hardware limitations. However, it is possible to access almost any Internet resource using e-mail. Simple e-mail commands can be used to access FTP, Usenet and the world wide web. Even if you do have full Internet access, using e-mail services can save you time and money. However, try to limit your data transfers to one megabyte per day, and don't swamp the servers with many requests at a time.

To retrieve web documents by e-mail, all you require is the URL which defines the address of the document. You can retrieve the text of that page by sending the email message

```
send URL
```

(substituting the URL for the site you wish to access for URL) to an Agora web-mail server (there are several located around the world).

To obtain a document (*Accessing The Internet By Email – Guide to Offline Internet Access*) listing these servers and with full instructions on how to retrieve www pages (and other services) by e-mail, send an e-mail message to:

mailbase@mailbase.ac.uk

In the body of your message, enter only this line:

```
send lis-iis e-access-inet.txt
```

Caching and mirror sites

The difficulty posed for networking staff who have to support a high demand for Internet access is considerable. Anyone who has tried to access a website in North America at 4pm knows how slow the response time can be! While some of the reasons for this are discussed below (see Common problems), one technique which helps to improve both the response time for Web end-users, and also reduces the network loading, is caching. The idea is to enable a local server to keep copies of the web pages that have recently been browsed. The next time someone else wishes to access that resource, the browser can retrieve its pages from the cache rather than returning to the remote server. In addition to easing network congestion, this can save on bandwidth costs.

Occasionally caching can create a problem if the pages you are looking for are updated several times a day (for example news or sports results) and the copy in the cache does not reflect this. However, it is possible to retrieve the most recent copy of a document by clicking on the 'Reload' button on your browser.

Many organizations block access from the Internet to their network(s). This prevents people outside the organization from gaining access to sensitive information – the mechanism used to achieve this is known as a *firewall*. Where organizations have a firewall in place, it may be necessary to go through a *proxy server* before connecting to the Internet. Proxy servers provide a cache (see above) of items available on remote servers. Proxy settings and caches can affect access to electronic journals and databases; your IT support staff should be able to advise.

Mirror sites are an alternative means of conserving bandwidth and speeding up retrieval. A mirror service is an exact copy of a complete website, software or files held in another geographical location. Publishers of electronic journals may have mirror sites for the Americas, Europe and Asia, for example. UKOLN offers mirrors of several library and information science journals at:

http://mirrored.ukoln.ac.uk/lis-journals/

Common problems

Some problems you may encounter when using a browser to access the web include the following messages:

- ★ *Error 404* – 'Not found' – is possibly the most common error message. It means that the document you requested cannot be found on the server. The URL may have been typed in wrongly, or the web pages moved to another server or removed from the web altogether. Alternatively, the web server you are trying to reach may be temporarily inaccessible – it is always worth trying later or the following day.
- ★ *Error 400* is a 'bad request', which means that something is wrong with the URL you typed. It may be that the server you're contacting doesn't recognize the document you're asking for or you may not be authorized to access it.
- ★ *Server timed out*: sometimes error messages are caused when the server you are trying to reach is too busy and you may receive this message. If this is the case, you should try again at a less busy time (normally mornings and weekends). In extreme cases, it can be worth clearing the cache on your local machine.
- ★ *Connection refused by host*: this means that you may not be allowed to access the document or site. This is normally because it is password-protected or

restricted to access from a particular domain. This is similar to *Error 403 – 'Forbidden'*.

★ *Failed DNS lookup*: means that the DNS or domain name system (which maintains a database for converting between domain names and IP addresses) cannot connect from the URL to a valid Internet address. This can be the result of a mistyped URL (specifically, a mistyped host name) or a harmless 'blip'. This can often be resolved by using the Reload button. If there is still a problem, it can be worth trying to connect an hour or so later.

If pages take a long time to load, there are various explanations: your local network or one of the networks used to connect to the required site may be busy (often described as a bandwidth problem), or the remote server may not be able to cope with the number of 'hits' it is receiving. It is always worth switching off the images option in your browser to speed up the load time, or trying to reconnect at a different time, preferably in the morning in the UK.

HTML coding can get garbled or links in a page may have been mistyped by the author – which will mean the intended page is not retrieved; in such cases it can be worth trying to modify the URL. This might involve substituting lower for upper case, a hyphen for an underscore character or vice versa. To see if the site is live, try going up one level (deleting the last part of the URL to the nearest slash), then check to see if there is a link to the document you are looking for.

The problem of accessibility has been touched on in Chapter 1 and in the discussion on browsers. If you use older browser software, you may find that you are unable to access some websites because they use Java. Java is a computer programming language that can be used to create complex applications on the web (animations, simulations and multimedia). Further information on Java can be found at:

http://www.sun.com/java/ or **http://www.javaworld.com/**

and on pages 202–3. Further information on connection difficulties and error messages is available at:

http://www.livinginternet.com/w/wt.htm

Telnet

Telnet is the basic Internet command used to make a simple connection to a computer somewhere. Typically this computer will have some sort of large searchable database, such as a library catalogue, a collection of references on a subject or statistical information. Many sources that originally used telnet access are now on the web so that use of telnet has become rarer.

The command is in the form:

```
telnet <address>
```

For example, you type:

```
telnet bcmsv.leeds.ac.uk
```

for an English verse collection at Leeds University.

If you use a graphical environment like Windows on your PC you may have an icon for telnet to double-click; a dialog box will then open in which you can enter the address. Alternatively, with a web browser enter the URL:

telnet://bcmsv.leeds.ac.uk

Occasionally you will also have to enter a user name or password, but you will normally be shown on the screen what this is. It will be the same for everyone and for a library catalogue may be something difficult like 'library'!

You may also be asked for a terminal type, perhaps with a list to choose from. Unless you know otherwise, reply `VT100`. The terminal type affects the screen layout, so if the layout is not right – for example, if it contains garbled characters – then you have the wrong terminal type.

If you have telnet software on your machine (a telnet 'client', in the jargon) then it will open in a window with drop-down menus for commands. You may need little other than the File/Exit command for when you are not disconnected automatically from the service you are using. Some software has commands from the keyboards. The most likely ones are:

- ★ `CONTROL-B` to send a break or interrupt command to the remote system if you need to stop some process, perhaps because you have made a mistake
- ★ `CONTROL-Q` to quit from telnet.

Telnet merely makes a connection to a computer – it has no search capability – and you will find that the databases you connect to with telnet may all be different in the way they work. You will probably need some instructions on how to use them, but these should be available online.

There is no complete directory of addresses of 'telnetable' resources, but a useful route to many, including bulletin boards, library catalogues from many countries and subject databases, is *Hytelnet* at:

http://www.lights.com/hytelnet/

This gives you lists from which you can connect to the service you want.

File transfer protocol

File transfer protocol, usually abbreviated to FTP, and sometimes known as anonymous FTP, was one of the first ways of using the Internet to transfer files between computers. Though other techniques can be used, FTP is still important. It is used much less for text than it once was because of the ease with which the web deals with text, but it remains a much faster way of transferring software, data collections and images between machines. Typically it can be ten times faster, which can be significant if you are using a slow dial-up connection, so you may want to use it to obtain such files for yourself or to advise users how to do so.

Until fairly recently the only way to use FTP was with a separate FTP program, but now a graphical web browser does the job more simply. It will sometimes use FTP without you knowing, for example if you download something such as software to your machine, but at other times you will need to go through a slightly more lengthy process.

Finding FTP files

You will come across references to FTP files in printed publications and on the Internet itself. Usually you will know where to get them, but if you have only the name of the file you will need to find a location.

Lists include:

Lycos
http://ftpsearch.lycos.com/

Monster FTP sites list
http://hoohoo.ncsa.uiuc.edu/ftp

Registry of FTP mirror sites on JANET
http://www.ftpregistry.mcc.ac.uk/
which lists overseas sites that are mirrored (copied) in the UK.

If the file is a program you can try a software archive like *Tucows*:
http://www.tucows.com/Europe.html
or *Jumbo*:
http://www.jumbo.com/
Otherwise use the Archie service.

Archie

Archie provides access to an index of millions of files stored in over 1500 archives across the world. You can search it for a particular file name, or in a very rudimentary way by subject for specific words that might appear in the name or sometimes in a description.

With a web browser use the ArchiePlex service at:

http://archie.emnet.co.uk/forms.html

You then simply fill in a box with the file name, and a list is returned with live links to the archive sites so that you can retrieve the file immediately by clicking.

Procedures

We will assume you are looking for an update to the McAfee Virus Scan software called update4076.zip which you know can be found at the URL:

ftp://ftp.mcafee.com/pub/antivirus/datfiles/update/update4076.zip

(Files are held in a hierarchy of directories – **pub** means public.)

With a browser like Netscape or a Windows FTP program like WS_FTP or RapidFiler getting files is simple.

In Netscape or Explorer you merely edit the Go To box or use the Open button and key the URL to get directly to the file you want. (Normally Netscape will automate the logon procedure, but occasionally you may need to enter the user name: `anonymous` and your e-mail address as the password.) You will then be able to save it, usually to wherever you want. However, there may be associated readme or help files or you may want to browse up and down directories to see what else is available; therefore it may be better to omit the file name so as to connect to the directory containing the file. Here the list of files is displayed, showing the name, file size, date created, etc. You then select any required.

With FTP software you can put in the full file path (the URL without the filename) or you may have to navigate the hierarchy of files to the directory and then select the file to save.

Older versions of FTP software, such as those using the MS-DOS operating system that predated Windows, require a more cumbersome procedure needing commands to be keyed in to list directories or choose files to be retrieved. You are unlikely to have to use this.

Compression

Many files available by FTP are in a compressed form – that is, they have been processed to reduce their size so as to decrease storage needs and speed up transfer. They then have to be uncompressed after transfer.

Filenames ending in *.zip* or *.z*, *.tar* or *.zoo* indicate compressed files.

Normally if your browser has the appropriate helper applications configured you should be able to decompress the files once they have been retrieved by clicking on **Extract**. However you may need to run a decompression program like PKZip or WinZip. Such programs may exist on your local system.

If in any doubt about what to do, contact your IT help.

5

Searching for information

- ★ Boolean and other concepts for searching
- ★ World wide web search tools
- ★ Searching discussion lists and newsgroup message archives
- ★ Search tool collections

Searching is a key approach to using the Internet, but its appropriateness in particular circumstances needs to be recognized: browsing sources, as discussed in the next chapter, is often more fruitful. It is not possible to 'search the Internet' in the sense of easily searching everything there is: it is more a matter of searching various parts. Thus you might search:

- ★ the general or specialist collections of millions of web pages: the web search engines
- ★ discussion list archives
- ★ Usenet newsgroup archives
- ★ e-mail address directories
- ★ subject databases like *PubMed* or *Research Index*
- ★ particular websites, such as the UK Government site
- ★ frequently asked questions (FAQs) on a subject
- ★ software archives
- ★ archives of data or images.

Before looking at specific sources, we need to look at some of the principles involved.

Concepts

To use any of these search facilities you need to understand the concepts used. You will be familiar with some of these if you have used CD-ROMs or other electronic databases.

Boolean logic

Of most importance is the use of AND, OR and NOT (Boolean logic).

- ★ Use AND to join concepts to make a search more specific. You want all the words to be present, eg `oil AND pollution AND north AND sea`.
- ★ Use OR to widen the search when you want any of a set of words to be present, or specify synonyms, eg `marine OR ocean OR sea`.
- ★ Use NOT to exclude words, eg `pollution NOT air`.

You can create more complex searches by using brackets, eg `oil AND pollution AND (sea OR ocean OR marine)`.

Some services may ask you to enter search terms (or keywords) in a box without making clear whether it will use AND or OR in searching, so you need to find out first. Some services require you to type AND or OR, others to indicate if you want 'all words' or 'any words' by checking (clicking) a box or by choosing from a menu. Some use + or – as alternative commands, though sometimes you are instructed to place + before a word that must appear in retrieved items; as if you would include a term you didn't want!

Truncation

The ability to search on part of a word so as to find material on similar words can simplify searching. So `medic` (may be input as `medic%`, `medic?` or `medic*`) will find material containing the words 'medical' or 'medicine'. This process is known as truncation, word stemming or using a wildcard. Some services truncate automatically, which can be a nuisance.

Fields

For large databases of textual material it is useful if you can restrict your search to a particular part (or field) of the information on the database, such as the document title, the summary (or abstract), index terms, or the URL for Internet resources, so as to get more accurate results. So if you are just trying to find a URL for a particular organization, for example, limiting the search on the organization's name to the URL field should give a more rapid result. Specialist databases might have other choices, for example a software collection would have a field for the operating system for each software package.

Entering terms

Many services are searching very large databases – those for the web are looking through millions of pages – so any words you look for may appear thousands of times. While a search for an uncommon name would probably find a small number of useful items, it is not a good idea to look for a single common term or phrase such as 'AIDS' or 'global warming' without being more precise, unless you are willing to plough through thousands of references. (The first example would also usually find references containing the word 'aids'.) In such instances a subject collection may be more useful. Conversely having too many search terms might produce nothing, when a slightly broader search would be helpful.

The context of the words you want may be wrong too, so a search for 'Craig Bruce' or 'Craig AND Bruce' might find Bruce Craig or a document that refers to, say, Bill Bruce and Craig someone else. However, some services do include a NEAR command to find words that are close together, and may allow you to search for phrases, either by enclosing the words in " " or by checking a box for this option.

Don't forget to consider alternative words or phrases. Thus, if you wanted to find out about fibre optics (used for computer and telephone network cables), you would need to take account of the US spelling 'fiber' and the phrase 'optical fibres' which is also used.

Natural language

Some services are starting to offer natural language input so that users don't have to take account of Boolean terms or other devices, but merely say what they want and the search software translates this into a query. The interpretation is not always correct and sometimes the system may respond with a need for clarification, eg 'Which Washington do you want?' A good example of natural language input is the *Ask Jeeves* web search service:

http://www.ask.co.uk

Scoring of results

Some web search services rank the search results with a scoring mechanism based on the position of the keywords within a document and their frequency, assuming that a document will be more relevant if the words appear in its title or frequently throughout the pages rather than occuring once at the end of the document. The results of your search will be displayed with the highest scoring first – maybe showing a numerical value with a maximum of 1.0, 1000 or 100%. This process is not always effective, however, so do not assume that only the first ten or 20 sources retrieved will be of value. You may need to look further through the list. Moreover different techniques are used by different services so a site ranked high in one service may be much lower in others.

Use the instructions

Unfortunately you cannot assume that because you know how to use one service you can use the others – often services have their own way of doing things! Thus, when using a service, you should read the instructions carefully before entering the search terms. These may be on the search screen, or you may have to look for a 'help', 'info', 'about', 'tips' or 'instructions' option that calls up detailed guidance, maybe with examples. Many services have poor instructions compared with other electronic information products with which we are familar.

As a librarian you will appreciate the need at times to use a range of these features to search effectively, but users may not do so. They may find some of the concepts difficult and can have a tendency to do simple searches – one web search service found the average search used 1.7 terms. Conversely users may sometimes be precise, with too many terms, because they don't understand what it is they are searching and what sort of response to expect. The librarian's role is often to help the user make the best of a resource.

General world wide web search services

The general web search services (alternatively called search programs, search tools or search engines) are frequently assumed to be the starting-point for finding information on the Internet. Often they are, but at other times a subject directory like *Yahoo* or *BUBL LINK* or a specialist resource may be more appropriate. Yet all these services are limited in that they cannot search ftp archives, message archives, subject databases, library catalogues or services available by telnet, though they may include Usenet groups.

The world wide web is an ever-growing collection of information, unstructured compared with a bibliographic database, so there is no clearly defined 'web' for these services to search. They each create their own version of the web by using 'robot' or 'crawler' programs. These start from a basic list of web sources and follow the hyperlinks to other sources, recording in a database details of the pages they find. Different starting-points and robots that work in different ways mean that the databases created will be different in content. None is comprehensive in its coverage – the largest indexes only about a third of the available estimated one billion pages – and there is overlap between them. Similarly there are differences in the way these databases are indexed and searched. This explains why different search services do not give the same results in response to a given search request. It is thus important to look at any help files to see how they work and how to use them. They are most effective when searching for something precise, like the name of a person or organization, though a common name would need to be associated with a narrowing concept too.

Most have a fairly basic search, which might have some Boolean options, but there is usually a further page – maybe labelled 'Power' or 'Advanced' search – with fuller Boolean capabilities, field searching and so on.

Since the tools base searching mainly on words in the text of web pages, rather than on a specialist controlled index, they are likely to return hundreds (or even thousands) of items unless you try to be precise in what you look for. Even then you will still get some wholly irrelevant results. If you have used full-text databases, such as newspaper CD-ROMs, you will appreciate the difficulties. We should remember that they are intended for the average user and not librarians, so we cannot expect the search sophistication of a structured bibliographic database, especially if the service is free.

However, new techniques are being developed to move away from word searching. Some services try to take account of the popularity of sites and return a Top Ten of most requested sites to a query or rank highest those sites with the most links. *Google* (**http://www.google.com**) is an example of such a service. In other services website owners can pay for their site to be displayed first.

Examples

There are many different search services, and new ones appear all the time, usually claiming to be bigger, faster and more effective than existing ones. At present the most useful ones are:

AltaVista
http://www.altavista.com/

Excite
http://www.excite.co.uk/

Hotbot
http://www.hotbot.com/

Infoseek
http://www.infoseek.com/

Lycos
http://www.lycos.co.uk/

Northern Light
http://www.northernlight.com/

Their key features are shown in Table 5.1, which can also be found at:
http://www.unn.ac.uk/features.htm

There is no 'best' search service since there are possibly a billion pages on the web and no service at the time of writing indexes more than around 300 million pages. Most of the services have other searchable sources, such as e-mail addresses (noted in Chapter 3) and yellow pages, a subject directory of resources and other features like news and online shopping. Northern Light also has a database of electronic journal articles, but you have to pay to retrieve the full text of these.

Services with extra resources are trying to be the only entry point – or 'portal' – to the Internet that a user needs, just as ISPs like *Freeserve* are too. Some of the services offered by ISPs incorporate the major search services, eg *Virgin.net* uses *Google*. As information professionals you will need to be more discerning than just to accept the first on offer, as this convenience may not always be best for all circumstances. You may find you prefer one or two services over the others, expecially if you just want 'something' on a subject, or if you need to use a particular search feature, but for an effective search – to find a very precise piece of information or to find as much as possible – you will need to use a number of them.

Table 5.1 *Features of web search services*

	AltaVista	Excite	Google	Hotbot	Infoseek	Lycos	Northern Light
Other sources	Usenet, sounds, pictures	Usenet, news, e-mail, addresses	None	Usenet, sounds, pictures	Usenet, e-mail, addresses, news	Sounds, pictures	Journal articles
Implied OR, AND	Implied OR	Implied OR	Implied	Implied AND	Implied OR	Implied AND	Implied AND
+ or –	Yes	Yes	Yes	Yes	Yes	Yes	Yes
AND, OR, NOT	In Advanced Search	Yes	No	Yes	No	Yes	Yes
Fields	title, URL, text, etc	No	No	title, domain, etc	title, URL, etc	URL, title, text, etc	title, text, URL, etc
Truncation	Uses *	No	No	Uses *	No	No	Uses *
Adjacency (phrase)	Uses " "	Uses " "	Uses " "	Uses " " or from menu	Uses " "	Uses " " or from menu	Uses " "
Proximity	Uses NEAR	No	No	No	No	Uses NEAR	No

Notes

'Other sources'. The service may search other Internet sources as well as the world wide web pages, most commonly the message archives of Usenet newsgroups. Many also link to services providing e-mail address directories, company information, and so on and may have a directory of Internet resources arranged by subject.

'Implied OR, AND'. Search words will be automatically OR'd together to look for pages with *any* of the words or AND'd to look for pages containing *all* of them.

' + and –'. Terms that must be present can be prefixed with + (the 'require' symbol). Those that must not be present can be indicated with – ('reject').

'AND, OR, NOT'. Terms can be linked with these Boolean operators as described above. Some services have options, such as 'all these words', 'any of these words' with the same purpose.

'Fields'. You can limit searching to words in page titles, URLs or maybe to particular subjects or countries. These facilities may appear in an 'advanced' or 'power' option.

'Adjacency'. A user can specify that words must be next to each other, as in a phrase or person's name. Sometimes there is a menu option to look for a phrase.

'Proximity'. A user can ensure that search words are near each other, eg in the same sentence or within a certain number of words.

Metasearch services

These are services that search most of the general services from one search screen, so that you can avoid having to connect to lots of them. They include:

Dogpile
http://www.dogpile.com/

Metacrawler
http://www.metacrawler.com/

Mamma
http://www.mamma.com/

They can be fast compared with searching services separately, but may have limits on the number of items returned from each service and the common search screen means you do not have the flexibility of searching offered when using the different services directly. They are best for single word or phrase searches.

Regional search services

The general web search services above are all USA-based and while they do have a worldwide coverage they tend to be dominated by USA sources, though Excite and Lycos do have British versions. If you want a more limited coverage geographically – say to find details of a German company or information that must relate to Britain – then a UK or European service may have a better coverage or simply be easier to use. These services limit to the country domain in a web address, eg **.uk**, so will not pick up sites using the international .com domain. The major examples are:

UKMax
http://www.ukmax.com/

Search UK
http:// searchuk.com/

EuroFerret
http://www.euroferret.co.uk/

Euroseek
http://www.euroseek.net/

For other countries see the geographically arranged list at:
http://bubl.ac.uk/searches/countries/

Multimedia sources

A growing number of services now offer a facility to search the web for sound files and images. These are not always very accurate for images, because most have to search for words in captions, web page titles and the text of pages containing the image, since there is rarely any accurate description of the image to use.

General services like *AltaVista*, *Hotbot*, *Lycos* and *Mamma* have options for sounds and pictures and specialist ones include:

Ditto.com
http://ditto.com/

Image surfer
http://isurf.interpix.com/
for still pictures.

WebSEEk
http://disney.ctr.columbia.edu/webseek
for still pictures and video.

Whoopie!
http://www.whoopie.com/
for audio and video.

These also allow you to browse by subject.

Subject search services

There are a number of services that search only web pages in particular subject areas, for example:

Artsearch
http://www.artsearch.net/

Energysearch
http://www.energysearch.com/

Law crawler
http://www.lawcrawler.com/

Mathsearch
http://www.maths.usyd.edu.au:8000/MathSearch.html

UK engineering search engine
http://www.eevl.ac.uk/uksearch.html
Others can be found in the subject gateways noted in Chapter 6 and in the search tool collections listed below.

Newsgroups and discussion lists

Discussion lists and newsgroups were discussed in Chapter 3 and though messages might seem ephemeral, they are normally stored for a while, and can be a valuable source of up-to-date practical information and news. There are various ways to search archives for many of these, though unfortunately not for all discussion lists. If you are thinking of sending a query to a list it may be helpful to check the archives first.

The UK Mailbase service
http://www.mailbase.ac.uk/
keeps two years' messages for each of its lists. These can be browsed and specific lists or groups of lists can be searched. The archives allow direct connection to any Internet sources quoted in messages. Extensive documentation is available.

Some of the lists using the Listserv mailing program have set up web-based searchable databases of messages while others merely provide a batch search of archives – that is, you send a message with your search requirement and receive an e-mail response with the results. The search facilities available should be made clear when you join a list.

The archives of newsgroups can be searched using various web services. Long established is *Deja.com*:
http://www.deja.com/usenet
and equally useful is *RemarQ*:
http://www.remarq.com/
A Usenet option is also offered by a number of the web search services discussed in the previous section (see Table 5.1). They may have different search facilities, and you need to check their 'help' files to see how much of Usenet is

covered and how far back they search.

The FAQs included in many newsgroups were mentioned in Chapter 3.

Search tool collections

There are various collections of search services you can use that can make it easier to remember what is available. They usually link to general and subject web search services and e-mail address directories, and maybe to subject collections, software archives and 'what's new' services too. Sometimes, however, they are just long lists that may confuse you, and they often give insufficient guidance on the use of services.

Graphical browsers used to access the web usually have a search option like Netscape's 'Net Search' and Internet Explorer's 'Go/Search the web' buttons that link to a variety of services.

A good selective collection is the

Scout Toolkit

http://www.ilrt.bris.ac.uk/mirrors/scout/toolkit

from InterNIC, the US Internet services organization, which covers browsers, searching tools, subject collections and what's new sources.

Search centre

http://www.tka.co.uk/search

has a business focus and covers web pages, files, software and people.

BIG Search Engine Index

http://www.search-engine-index.co.uk/search.htm

has a large list of sources, but may be confusing to use.

WebPlaces Internet Search Guide

http://www.webplaces.com/

covers a very wide range of services.

Subjects

There are other services that concentrate on identifying subject databases like *Pub Med* or *RAM* (manufacturing) that are not searched by the general web search services.

Direct Search
http://gwis2.circ.gwu.edu/~gprice/direct.htm
is produced by a librarian at George Washington University and has a huge number of specialist resources, especially in business and politics.

Others with a less academic content are:

Allsearchengines.com
http://www.allsearchengines.com/

The Big Hub
http://www.thebighub.com/

Invisible web
http://www.invisibleweb.com/

Lycos searchable databases
http://dir.lycos.com/Reference/Searchable_Databases/

The subject directories in Chapter 6 will also direct you to appropriate searchable sources.

6

Browsing for subject information

- ★ Multidisciplinary subject directories
  - UK
  - Non-UK
- ★ Portals and directory listings
- ★ Subject gateways and hubs
  - Resource Discovery Network
- ★ Subject resource guides

There are two main ways to track information on the Internet: searching using a search engine or other retrieval tool (see Chapter 5), or browsing in an Internet subject directory or gateway, which this chapter deals with. Parallel with the development of more sophisticated Internet retrieval tools have been attempts to organize the Internet intellectually. In response to the need for better subject access to Internet resources, various services have been set up to facilitate this – the major ones are discussed in this chapter and they are also extensively referred to in the resource guides in Part 2.

The earliest collections of resources organized by subject were known as subject trees. These offered a method of organizing related resources without regard to their physical location, and normally included direct links to the listed resources. Nowadays they are usually referred to as subject gateways, subject collections or directories, and may either be multidisciplinary or focus on a particular subject area. They are ideally suited to browsing for information, when you wish to know what resources are available in a specific subject area.

The subject gateways tend to evaluate and describe Internet resources, but other services simply add links to hierarchical menus (sometimes known as 'channels'). An increasing number of websites have developed the *portal* concept – incorporating a directory of Internet sites along with news feeds, free e-mail and other tools. A portal can be a valuable starting-point for new Internet users, but the impetus for development is usually commercial and supported by advertising.

Portals are intended as a one-stop shop or department store to keep users at that site to view the adverts or use the shopping facilities. They have limitations for information professionals who will want to develop their own resource collections using local web pages and bookmarks as well as portals; they can also be slow to load and poorly designed. Home pages for the major consumer-oriented Internet Service Providers (eg *Freeserve*, *Virgin.net*) are portals.

Traffick: the Guide to Portals
http://www.traffick.com/
follows web portal trends with regular columns, news, comparisons, tools, tutorials, specialized reports and statistics.

Multidisciplinary subject directories

The sites below include an element of annotation – with brief descriptions or reviews of resources, rather than mere links.

UK directories

BUBL Link
http://www.bubl.ac.uk/Link/
is a long-established project that selects, organizes and describes high-quality resources of academic relevance.

EARLweb
http://www.earl.org.uk/earlweb/index.html
is a ready reference to information on the Internet for public library staff. Sections comprise: the global library, lifelong learning, science and technology, the citizen in society, imagination and memory, the online enquiry desk, business intelligence and the public librarian.

Non-UK directories

About.com

http://home.about.com/index.htm

A network of sites including over 700 highly targeted 'environments', or subject areas, with annotations. Many leisure areas are covered, and the section on Internet/online is valuable for beginners.

AlphaSearch

http://www.calvin.edu/library/searreso/internet/as/

provides instant access to hundreds of gateway sites. It offers both searching and browsing facilities by discipline and/or resource type. All sites included in AlphaSearch have been evaluated for content, academic appropriateness and currency.

InfoMine

http://lib-www.ucr.edu/

offers searching and browsing in its collection of 20,000 academically valuable resources in a whole range of subject areas. Internet/web resources include databases, electronic journals, electronic books, bulletin boards, listservs, online library catalogs, articles and directories of researchers.

Scout Report Signpost

http://www.signpost.org/signpost/

contains Internet resources chosen by the editorial staff of the *Scout Report* (a series of electronic newsletters listing new resources):

http://www.ilrt.bris.ac.uk/mirrors/scout/report/sr/about.html

which have been catalogued and organized for efficient browsing and searching.

Top of the Web

http://www.december.com/web/top.html

John December nominates his 'top five' resources in the following categories: art, business, computers, education, entertainment, government, humanities, keywords, lookup, marketing, money, news, people, science, software and subjects.

The World-Wide Web Virtual Library was the first subject-based collection of web resources, predating the development of graphical browsers for the world wide web. It is a distributed subject catalogue, created by volunteers from around the world, who are often experts in their own field. Note that it does not cover all subject areas. The URL for the UK mirror site is:

http://www.mth.uea.ac.uk/VL/Home.html
but you will find that specific subject sections are based wherever they are maintained.

Portals and directory listings

The resources below tend to include a search facility (see Chapter 5) in addition to the opportunity to browse by subject. To use these services to their full potential, it is important to read any help or information files that they may provide. These will tend to discuss search strategies, Boolean syntax and any personalization options offered.

Britannica.com
http://www.britannica.com/
lets users simultaneously search the complete, updated *Encyclopædia Britannica*, reviews of more than 125,000 websites, articles from leading magazines, and related books.

Excite UK
http://www.excite.co/uk/
is a large database of Internet resources, which offers two approaches to locating information: a search facility and channels, which are organized by topic in a many-tiered hierarchy.

Galaxy
http://www.einet.net/galaxy.html
provides ten subject categories, each with subheadings, to browse.

Looksmart UK
http://www.looksmart.co.uk/
provides keyword search, category-based directory and interactive search services.

Lycos UK
http://www.lycos.co.uk/
provides a browsable directory (*Webguides*) and a range of search options. *Lycos* promotes Family Safe Software, and provides users with subsidized software tools to filter out offensive content.

Magellan
http://magellan.excite.com/
is an online directory with brief annotations about each resource listed in its 18 browsable subject categories. *Magellan* is owned by *Excite*.

UK Directory
http://www.ukdirectory.com/
aims to provide a comprehensive guide to everything on the web in the UK.

UK Index
http://www.ukindex.co.uk/index.html
does not offer a browsing facility, but the search facility can be combined with category searching and brief summaries of resources are provided.

WebCrawler
http://webcrawler.com/
is a search tool that also offers 19 channels for browsing Internet resources. *WebCrawler* is owned by *Excite*.

Yahoo! UK & Ireland
http://uk.yahoo.com/
is frequently talked about as a search tool, but is more accurately described as a virtual library or directory. Users can search the database to find information on the web, or browse down *Yahoo!*'s 14 hierarchical categories.

Subject gateways and hubs

Subject gateways collect and evaluate Internet resources in a particular subject area. The majority of these have an academic origin, and many are included in the *World-Wide Web Virtual Library*. A number of the Internet resources listed below are included in *Pinakes*, a website which aims to catalogue major subject gateways:
http://www.hw.ac.uk/libWWW/irn/pinakes/pinakes.html
The majority of the gateways listed below aim to provide a comprehensive list of relevant UK-based sources in their subject area, as well as a guide to high-quality international networked resources. Such gateways normally evaluate, select and describe the resources they include and in many cases it is possible to browse the resource descriptions before connecting directly to the resource itself. A search facility, allowing keyword searching of the descriptions and

other information, is normally available. Most of these sites will also include a 'what's new' facility, background information on the project, and possibly additional subject services.

In the UK, a number of subject gateways were funded through eLib, the Electronic Libraries Programme; these are marked below with an *. During 2000, many of these will be incorporated into the *Resource Discovery Network* (see below).

ADAM – art, design, architecture and media*
http://adam.ac.uk/

AERADE – aerospace and defence
http://aerade.cranfield.ac.uk/

Biz/ed – economics and business*
http://www.bizednet.bris.ac.uk/

Business Information Sources on the Internet
http://www.dis.strath.ac.uk/business/index.html

CAIN – conflict studies*
http://cain.ulst.ac.uk/

Chemdex – chemistry
http://www.chemdex.org/

EEVL – engineering*
http://eevl.ac.uk/

ELDIS – development and the environment
http://nt1.ids.ac.uk/eldis

*History**
http://ihr.sas.ac.uk/

Lingu@NET – language learning
http://vtc.ngfl.gov.uk/resource/linguanet/index.html

OMNI – biomedicine*
http://omni.ac.uk/

Port – maritime studies
http://www.port.nmm.ac.uk/

RUDI – urban design*
http://rudi.herts.ac.uk/

psi-com – public understanding of science
http://www.psci-com.org.uk/

SOSIG – social sciences, business and law*
http://sosig.ac.uk/

The *Resource Discovery Network* (RDN)

The *Resource Discovery Network* (RDN)
http://www.rdn.ac.uk/
is a UK resource being developed to carry forward the subject gateway concept. It will cover academic subjects on a faculty hub basis, with a number of subject gateways clustered round each hub. Most RDN hubs will be launched in Summer 2000 and at present comprise:

BIOME – health and life sciences
http://biome.ac.uk/

EMC – engineering, mathematics and computing
http://www.emc.ac.uk/

Humbul – humanities
http://www.humbul.ac.uk/

PSIgate – physical sciences
http://www.psigate.ac.uk/

SOSIG – social sciences, business and law
http://www.sosig.ac.uk/

Subject resource guides

In addition to gateways, directories and portals which provide links to sites in a particular subject area, there have been many guides created which describe the full range of Internet resources (websites, discussion lists, newsgroups, FTP archives, etc) for a specific topic. These guides normally include annotations or comments, and are particularly valuable if the author is an authority on the topic. If a guide has been produced for a topic of interest to you, then much of the preliminary browsing has already been done for you – provided that the guide is comprehensive and is kept up-to-date!

The major collection of these guides is the *Argus Clearinghouse*:

http://www.clearinghouse.net/

Unfortunately, guides are not available for every subject area and in some cases are merely lists of discussion lists. One useful feature of the *Clearinghouse* is that it provides the date on which a guide was last updated and contact details for the author.

PART 2

Guide to resources

Introduction

This guide aims to provide an introduction to the range of resources available on the Internet. It does not try to be comprehensive but attempts to show the reader the type and extent of online information available on subjects typically covered by public libraries. Resources are listed by topic and examples are given of the most typical type of website on each topic. Where possible links to directories listing other relevant resources have been included.

At the time of writing (June 2000) all the resources listed were current and their web addresses were correct. Unfortunately the Internet is a constantly developing medium and some of these resources may move or disappear over time.

7

Business and finance resources

- ★ News and current affairs
- ★ Associations and company information
- ★ Directories
- ★ UK business advice and resources
- ★ Personal finance
- ★ European economy
- ★ World economy
- ★ Employment and training

An enormous number of sites on the web are providing information on business and finance, from the latest share prices to worldwide taxation regulations. With this topic, though, the accuracy and currency of the information provided is especially important to the user, particularly in the case of the official government information and the market information that is available. Since up-to-date information in this subject area is so valuable, many of the relevant Internet services are subscription only, although some of these services may also provide a free introductory or 'taster' session, which can be used before a subscription is required. The current UK Government's agenda recognizes that access to informed and up-to-date information resources are vital if we are to cope effectively with economic changes and the transformations that the traditional workplace is undergoing. As well as information, you will find an increasing number of forms, from government departments and regulatory bodies, such as the Inland Revenue, that can be downloaded or completed and submitted online.

This chapter concentrates mainly on the provision of information, rather than the business and financial transactions and e-commerce that is now prevalent over the Internet. Individual company websites have not been included, but can be found via the directories listed.

News and current affairs

Many well-established print-based news publications will have a presence on the Internet, although they may be selective in the coverage provided online compared with the printed version. Some sites may be updated several times during the day. News items include a mixture of news stories, feature articles, market and share price reports and press releases.

Financial Times
http://www.ft.com/
An e-mail newsletter delivers weekly round-ups of financial news to your desktop. The site also include tools for managing your time and work, such as a calendar and e-mail facilities.

The Economist
http://www.economist.com/
Articles from the current edition and a searchable archive of articles since 1995.

BBC Business News
http://news.bbc.co.uk/hi/english/business/default.htm
News and articles plus a number of features, including video and audio broadcasts of various BBC programmes and Marketwatch, which will sit on your desktop and deliver up-to-date market news from the FTSE 100 and Dow Jones and prices of popular shares.

Department of Trade and Industry
http://www.dti.gov.uk/
A huge site containing much information as well as links to related sites. Press releases include links to external press releases from other related organizations, eg Companies House and the Equal Opportunities Commission, as well as other government ministries and offices. Also includes full text of ministerial speeches.

HM Treasury
http://www.hm-treasury.gov.uk/
Includes information on recent budgets.

FTSE International

http://www.ftse.com/

The website contains a selection of material and indices produced by the FTSE International.

Associations and company information

Most organizations now have a presence on the web, although the extent and range of information available on their websites will vary. Some, such as the TUC, have taken advantage of the web environment to present the information they offer on their website in an innovative way, whilst on other websites you may find little more than contact details for further enquiries.

Trades Union Congress

http://www.tuc.org.uk/

The TUC have arranged their website as a virtual building with floors divided up by the type of user and their information needs. Find out your rights at work or move up a floor and search the many employment-related publications online.

Confederation of British Industry

http://www.cbi.org.uk/

Information for employers.

Equal Opportunities Commission

http://www.eoc.org.uk/

News and information on the work of the Commission.

Companies House

http://www.companies-house.gov.uk/

As well as providing a range of its advice booklets online, the Companies House site provides limited access to its main databases. Currently free access is available to its Index of Basic Company Information and Register of Disqualified Directors.

Carol World

http://www.carol.co.uk/

Provides a selection of worldwide company reports online.

Directories

There are many business and finance-specific directories on the Internet and these are a good place to start searching for information. Some services, such as the *Biz/ed* subject gateway, evaluate all the resources that they make available.

Biz/ed
http://www.bized.ac.uk/
Biz/ed is a subject gateway for business and economics. It is designed for use by students and their teachers, but will be of general use also. All the sites listed on the gateway have been selected by the service providers in accordance with the service's quality criteria. Abstracts of all resources included are provided. The site includes learning materials which support many aspects of the business studies and economics curricula. The Virtual Factory and Virtual Economy are large-scale learning resources that give an opportunity for applying business studies theory to real-world business and economic situations.

Business Information Sources on the Internet
http:/www.dis.strath.ac.uk/business/
This site aims to be a selective guide to business resources on the Internet, with some emphasis on UK sites. Sites are included according to a selection policy. The scope and coverage of the site is described.

Yahoo's Business and Economy Directory
http://uk.dir.yahoo.com/Business_and_Economy/
As well as being a search engine, Yahoo arranges resources in hierarchical subject collections. You can choose between searching and browsing UK-only sites or worldwide sites selected by subject area.

Dow Jones Business Directory
http://bd.dowjones.com/
Sites are evaluated for content, speed, navigation and design. Descriptions of each site include 'key reasons to use this site'.

CorporateInformation
http://www.corporateinformation.com/
A huge site and a good place to start from to find information on specific private and publicly owned companies worldwide.

UK business advice and resources

Business Matters

http://www.business.knowledge.com/

A site designed for (and by) people starting up their own companies. Provides advice and sources of further information.

Business Link

http://www.businesslink.co.uk/

Provides access to a range of business support opportunities, services and information. Includes contact details for local *Business Link* offices.

Inland Revenue

http://www.inlandrevenue.gov.uk/

Regularly updated information including key dates for self assessment taxation returns, etc. A range of the Inland Revenue's forms, leaflets and booklets are available to download directly from the site.

HM Customs & Excise

http://www.hmce.gov.uk/

Includes general information about HM Customs & Excise as well as public and business information. Many of the department's leaflets and booklets are available.

Office for National Statistics

http://www.statistics.gov.uk/stats/ukinfigs/ukinfig.htm

The Office for National Statistics makes available a selected range of official statistics for the UK, including statistics on economic and financial trends and employment.

Department of Trade and Industry's Information Society Initiative

http://www.isi.gov.uk/

This Initiative aims to encourage businesses to take advantage of the explosion of new ways to access, use and send information. The site includes a large amount of information, aimed particularly at smaller UK companies that may have little knowledge of the potential of information and communications technologies within their business.

UK Equities Direct

http://www.hemscott.com/

Provides key financial data on many companies free of charge. Share prices are updated every 15 minutes. More detailed information is provided on a subscription-only service.

Personal finance

Personal banking and finance are gradually moving out of the High Street as banks and financial institutions develop phone and online services for their customers. And as the range of available financial products increases, people need to know more about the financial options available to them.

MoneyWorld
http://www.moneyworld.co.uk/
A comprehensive site providing personal finance information. Contains a useful glossary and selection of guides to FAQs on personal finance matters.

The Motley Fool
http://www.fool.co.uk/
Aims to 'educate, amuse and enrich' you in the ways of personal finance and investing. As well as news and the latest market information, features include My Portfolio, which allows you to track your real (or fantasy) stocks, and Stock Ideas, which highlights investment opportunities.

Interactive Investor
http://www.iii.co.uk/
Provides information on investments and tools to help you manage and monitor your interests. You can also e-mail questions to a panel of experts. Many of the services do require that you register, but this is free of charge.

This is Money
http://www.thisismoney.com/
Personal finance news and information from the publishers of the *Daily Mail* and *Evening Standard*.

European economy

The Euro: Now in Business
http://www.euro.gov.uk/
The official UK government website providing information for UK businesses getting to grips with the Euro.

Statistical Indicators from the Statistical Office of the European Communities
http://europa.eu.int/en/comm/eurostat/
Provides a selection of statistics and indicators on social and economic activities. Available in English, French and German.

The Euro – One Currency for Europe
http://europa.eu.int/euro/
The European Commission's Internet site dedicated to the Euro. The site has information in all 11 official languages of the European Union and also provides access to an electronic version of *Infeuro*, the Commission's own newsletter on the Euro, plus other sites with information on the single currency.

World economy

Foreign & Commonwealth Office
http://www.fco.gov.uk/trade/
Trade news and information from the Foreign & Commonwealth Office.

British Trade International
http://www.brittrade.com/
Advice for exporters and overseas market information from the Department of Trade and Industry and the Foreign & Commonwealth Office.

World Bank
http://www.worldbank.org/
The site includes reports on development topics, the operations and policies of the Bank and profiles of various regions and countries.

Employment and training

An increasing number of job vacancies are being advertised on the Internet, and in some cases this is the only place vacancies appear – particularly jobs in ICT. Many newspapers and journals have developed their situations vacant pages to allow users to make their CVs available on the site and have vacancies matching their employment profiles e-mailed directly to them on a regular basis.

The Guardian: jobs unlimited
http://www.jobsunlimited.co.uk/

You can browse vacancies in the governmental, charity and voluntary sectors as well as by subject area. You can register your job-hunting profile and receive vacancies matching your profile by e-mail.

New Scientist Jobs
http://www.newscientistjobs.com/
E-mails a selection of scientific-related vacancies to your desktop each week.

Jobsite
http://www.jobsite.co.uk/
For job-hunters and recruiters in all sectors. Job-seekers can complete an employment profile and targeted jobs are e-mailed directly to them daily.

NISS recruitment services and events
http://www.niss.ac.uk/cr/careers/recruit.html
Listing of links to graduate recruitment and careers sites.

Training and Enterprise Councils
http://www.tec.co.uk/
The site contains information on all UK TECs. Some regional TECs have their own websites that are accessible from here. The site also includes a discussion forum open to all.

UfI
http://www.ufiltd.co.uk/
The site currently provides information about the UfI initiative which aims to 'boost the competitiveness of business and the employability of individuals'. Provides location details for the developing *learndirect* network of local centres which are currently delivering courses in information technology and business and management skills.

8

Children's resources

- ★ Directories
- ★ Resources for the pre-school child
- ★ Homework resources
  - – Art
  - – Design and technology
  - – English
  - – Geography
  - – History
  - – Information technology
  - – Modern foreign languages
  - – Mathematics
  - – Music
  - – Science
- ★ Fun and games
- ★ Information for librarians and parents

The range, standard and type of online resources available for children is truly astounding. Using the Internet it is possible for a child to chat online live with an astronaut in space, e-mail a prime minister and share work and experiences with children all around the world. This section can only give a taster of the range of material available and should not be seen as a comprehensive guide to online resources. Many of the best sites for children have been developed for a US audience, but UK sites have been identified where possible. Children's sites, in particular, seem to use a high number of plug-ins as they often involve games and high levels of interactivity. For a library to make use of many of these sites they will need to have the latest versions of plug-ins like Flash and Shockwave installed.

Directories

The range of material available for children can be overwhelming both for adults and children. In order to help find the best resources there are a number of web directories designed purely for children – many of these directories have been developed by creditable organizations like the American Library Association.

Yahooligans
http://www.yahooligans.com/
Yahooligans is run by Yahoo!, one of the major Internet search engines. It is probably the most well-known directory of children's resources. Each resource in the directory has been assessed by *Yahooligans'* staff as being suitable for children to use. The directory is organized hierarchically and can also be keyword searched. The site is American and homework resources in particular have an American focus.

Great Sites for Kids from the American Library Association
http://www.ala.org/parentspage/greatsites/
The American Library Association has developed several directory sites for children – this site is the largest with over 700 websites. All the resources have been selected by children's librarians.

Teen Hoopla
http://www.ala.org/teenhoopla/
Good sites for teenagers, selected again by the American Library Association.

Ask Jeeves for Kids
http://www.ajkids.com/
A search engine aimed at children which allows them to ask it real questions rather than construct a search query.

Internet Public Library Youth Division
http://www.ipl.org/youth/
The Internet Public Library aims to be the public library of the Internet. It collects, classifies and organizes content on the Internet. It has a thriving children's and youth department which provides pointers to large numbers of useful Internet sites. Again, this site is primarily aimed at a US audience.

Internet Public Library Teen Division
http://www.ipl.org/teen/

KidsClick!

http://sunsite.berkeley.edu/KidsClick!/

A collection of resources for children put together by even more librarians.

Resources for the pre-school child

Many of the resources for young children involve sound and animation. Once again it is important for the library to have the latest versions of plug-ins installed and perhaps provide headphones as well.

Teletubbies

http://www.bbc.co.uk/education/teletubbies/

Say 'Eh-oh' to the online Teletubbies.

Little Animals Activity Centre

http://www.bbc.co.uk/education/laac/

Counting and learning games.

Learning Planet

http://www.learningplanet.com/kids.htm

Choose the preschool-k level for online activities which help children to learn to count (though with an American accent!).

Shoo Rayner

http://www.shoo-rayner.co.uk/

Shoo Rayner's Ginger Ninja on the web – a brilliant site which children will enjoy exploring – make sure that you explore it all.

Homework resources

The potential of the Internet to augment traditional learning resources is huge. The Internet allows children access to learning material from around the world. It is just as easy for a child to find out up-to-the-minute information from NASA as to borrow a book from the library about spaceships. There will be a growing use of online material in children's schoolwork as the Internet becomes a tool used daily in their lessons. Access to Internet resources in the library will also therefore become the norm as children become familiar with using it as an everyday text.

Homework resources have been organized into UK National Curriculum topic areas.

General homework resources

Directories of educational resources for children on the Internet are available in large numbers. The website of BBC Education is particularly useful as it points to external material which can be searched by National Curriculum area and age group. The BBC also provides many useful educational resources on its own site. Many of the other directories are aimed specifically at a US audience, but there are still many resources which would be useful to a British child.

BBC Education Web Guide
http://bbc.co.uk/plsql/education/webguide/pkg_main.p_home
The *BBC Education Web Guide* chooses the best websites for education. Subject specialists have written reviews on how to integrate each site into learning – both in the classroom and at home.

BBC Education Archive
http://www.bbc.co.uk/education/archive/
An easy way into the mass of educational resources available on the BBC site.

BBC Bitesize GCSE Revision
http://www.bbc.co.uk/education/revision/

Thinkquest
http://library.advanced.org/library/
A collection of educational resources developed by educators all around the world. Resources are usefully organized in a subject-type hierarchy which can also be keyword searched.

Fun Brain
http://www.funbrain.com/

StudyWeb
http://www.studyweb.com/

Letsfindout
http://www.letsfindout.com/
The knowledge adventure encyclopaedia – information on many topics easily available here.

Facts and Current Events – from KidsClick!
http://sunsite.berkeley.edu/KidsClick!/topfact.html

Collection of resources to things like newspapers, encyclopaedias, dictionaries and so on.

Homework Elephant
http://www.homeworkelephant.free-online.co.uk/
Hurrah – a UK-based resource!

Art

The @rt Room
http://www.arts.ufl.edu/art/rt_room/@rtroom_home.html
A virtual learning environment for exploring the world of art – aimed at children aged eight upward.

Art Attack
http://www.artattack.co.uk/
The interactive website from the children's TV programme of the same name.

Art for Kids
http://artforkids.miningco.com/
A collection of resources for children about art.

Design and technology

How Stuff Works
http://www.howstuffworks.com/
An extremely useful site which tells you how things work – topics range from engines to teeth cavities to light sabres.

WONKA
http://www.wonka.com/Home/wonka_home.html
Technology information hidden inside this fun site about Willy Wonka – blatant advertising though.

Design and Technology Online
http://www.dtonline.org/

Reinventing the Wheel
http://www.bbc.co.uk/education/wheel/
Interactive information from the BBC about technology and inventions.

English

Stories from the Web
http://hosted.ukoln.ac.uk/stories/
A public library project which is exploring how libraries can use the Internet to help children develop traditional and online literacy skills. Contains excerpts from major children's books and a number of online literature-based activities. Also has great Harry Potter activities.

Treasure Island
http://www.ukoln.ac.uk/services/treasure/
Created by UKOLN, this site provides information about the book *Treasure Island*. It draws upon resources about *Treasure Island* on the Internet in order to get children to learn more about the book. Online activities include a quiz and opportunities to review the book and design a pirate.

Resources for Young Writers
http://www.inkspot.com/young/
Links to resources for the budding young writer.

BookHive
http://www.bookhive.org/bookhive.htm
Book reviews galore, but primarily aimed at American children and so concentrates on American authors.

BBC Webguide – Children's Stories
http://www.bbc.co.uk/webguide/childrens/stories.shtml
Collection of links to sites for children about literature and stories.

Lord of the Flies
http://www.gerenser.com/lotf/index.html
This site provides lots of information about *Lord of the Flies*. There are many other sites which concentrate on a single novel or author in this way. These sites can be identified by searching one of the main search engines.

Geography

The Globe Programme in the UK
http://www.globe.org.uk/intro/pagepupil.html

GLOBE is an international environmental education project. Children in schools gather environmental data and share it worldwide using the Internet.

National Geographic

http://www.nationalgeographic.com/

The online version of the famous magazine. Includes a useful archive and interactive features designed for children.

World Environment Changes

http://www.bbc.co.uk/education/landmarks/

Looks at how five very different environments have changed as the human population has increased.

Exploring the Environment

http://www.cotf.edu/ete/modules/modules.html

Environment information developed with NASA.

Terraserver

http://terraserver.microsoft.com/

Free access to satellite images from space – some areas of the UK are covered. Provides links to free articles in Microsoft's *Encarta* encyclopaedia on the places shown in the images.

Volcanoes Online

http://library.advanced.org/17457/

Lots of volcanic facts!

Fun Factory from East of Scotland Water

http://www.esw.co.uk/funfactory/

Information and games about water.

Greatest Places Online

http://www.greatestplaces.org/

Beautifully presented information about the Amazon, Greenland, Iquazu, Madagascar, Namib, Okavango and Tibet.

Horus Website

http://www.horus.ics.org.eg/

Information about both modern and ancient Egypt.

History

BBC Online – History
http://www.bbc.co.uk/history/
The entry point to all the BBC's excellent online history resources.

Junior Parliament for the Under 12s
http://explore.parliament.uk/
An interactive way to learn about who does what and where in the Houses of Parliament.

The Romans
http://www.bbc.co.uk/education/romans/
Useful but dull information about the Roman Empire from the BBC – includes an interactive quiz though.

Modern World History
http://www.bbc.co.uk/education/modern/
A brilliant site about modern history concentrating mainly on World War 2. Contains interactive quizzes.

Tower of London
http://www.tower-of-london.com/
Ghost stories, interactive games, famous last words and of course the history of the Tower.

WW1 – Trenches on the Web
http://www.worldwar1.com/
Lots of information about the World War 1 – really aimed at adults though.

The World Wars in the Virtual Classroom
http://www.mrdowling.com/706wars.html
Facts children should know about the World Wars and links to other useful educational war material.

The Middle Ages
http://www.learner.org/exhibits/middleages/
Information about what it was like to live in the Middle Ages.

Empires Past
http://library.advanced.org/16325/

Information and games about the ancient empires of Egypt, China, Rome and the Aztecs.

The Viking Network Web
http://viking.no/
Lots of information about Vikings!

The Magna Carta
http://www.law.ou.edu/hist/magna.html
The full text available online.

EyeWitness – History Through the Eyes of Those Who Lived It
http://www.ibiscom.com/
First-person accounts of major historical events.

Information technology

Internet Safety Quiz for Kids
http://www.missingkids.com/quiz/internetquiz.html

Other useful IT resources can be found in Chapter 14.

Modern foreign languages

The Internet provides easy access to resources in many different languages. The selection of resources below gives an idea of the sort of material which is available on the web. Use one of the major search engines to find more specific material.

French Prime Minister's Site
http://www.premier-ministre.gouv.fr/GB/
Background information about how the government is structured in France.

Der Spiegel
http://www.spiegel.de/
Online version of the German magazine.

Leo English/German Dictionary
http://dict.leo.org/

BBC Education Languages
http://www.bbc.co.uk/education/languages/
Online language resources from the BBC.

BBC's Bitesize GCSE Resources
http://www.bbc.co.uk/education/schools/secondar.shtml#modlang

Mathematics

There are many educational and fun maths websites available. They cover all age ranges needs. Typically, like many educational resources, they have been developed for an American audience.

Megamaths
http://www.bbc.co.uk/education/megamaths/
A BBC-developed site which is aimed at 7–10-year-olds. It offers help with practising and testing timetables knowledge.

Maths File
http://www.bbc.co.uk/education/mathsfile/
This is aimed at Key Stage Three pupils and explores the relevant areas of the maths section of the National Curriculum.

This is Mega-Mathematics
http://www.c3.lanl.gov/mega-math/
This aims to bring unusual and important maths ideas into schools. It tries to make accessible and understandable the maths problems facing mathematicians today.

LCSI – Project Library – Math
http://www.microworlds.com/library/math/
This provides maths projects online.

Archimedes
http://www.mcs.drexel.edu/~crorres/Archimedes/contents.html
Information here about the most famous mathematician of them all.

Wognu Art – Brainwave
http://www.wognum.se/Brainwave/
Provides ten mathematical puzzles – how well will you do?

Totally Tessellated

http://library.advanced.org/16661/

An introduction to tessellation.

The Math Forum

http://www.askdrmath.com/

E-mail Dr Math your tricky trigonometry question.

Music

Hop Pop Town

http://www.kids-space.org/HPT/

Aims to encourage children to improvise musical sequences.

Music Education at Data Dragon

http://datadragon.com/education/

Online tutorials and guides to music.

StudyWeb – Music

http://www.studyweb.com/Music/

Large collection of links to educational music resources on the Internet.

Science

The Ultimate Dinosaur Links page

http://www.dinosaur.org/links.html

Over 200 links to dinosaur material on the Internet – whatever they want, it must be here somewhere.

Ocean Futures

http://www.oceanfutures.com/

Ocean Futures provides information about Keiko the killer whale who starred in *Free Willy*. Keiko is currently being prepared to be released back into the wild and this site provides weekly updates on how he's progressing.

Yuckiest Site on the Web

http://www.yucky.com/

A fun and educational site which concentrates on the more 'yucky' aspects of biology including bugs, worms and human bodily functions!

NASA for Kids
http://www.nasa.gov/kids.html

Arty the Part Time Astronaut
http://www.artyastro.com/
Lots of games about the solar system on this site.

MadSciNet
http://www.madsci.org/
MadSciNet is a resource which makes hundreds of scientists around the world available to children via the Internet. It answers questions in many areas, covering chemistry, physics, astronomy, engineering, computer science, earth sciences and the biological sciences.

PhysLINK
http://www.physlink.com/
Aims to provide comprehensive research and education tools to physicists, engineers, educators, students and all other curious minds.

SciCentral – K-12 Science
http://www.scicentral.com/K-12/
Extensive collection of science links for children, aimed primarily at a US audience.

Bizarre Stuff You Can Make in Your Kitchen
http://freeweb.pdq.net/headstrong/
Kitchen sink science and experiments.

The Exploritorium
http://www.exploratorium.edu/
The American Museum of Science, Art and Human Perception. The website is interactive and has many online exhibitions.

The Discovery Channel
http://www.discovery.com/
Lots of interesting material including a live webcam in a wedding chapel in Las Vegas – always entertaining if not always educational.

Natural History Museum – Interactive Fun
http://www.nhm.ac.uk/interactive.html
Educational things to do online.

National Science Museum – Online Features
http://www.nmsi.ac.uk/on-line/

Science in Action
http://www.bbc.co.uk/sia/

Secrets At Sea
http://www.secretsatsea.org/main.html
Solve the ocean-themed mystery.

Fun and games

The Internet isn't just for education and there are lots of purely fun resources available for children. Listed below is just a small selection.

Yahooligans – Downloader Pictures
http://www.yahooligans.com/Downloader/Pictures/
A useful place to find great pictures of all sorts of things.

Kids Mysteries: The Case.com for kids
http://www.thecase.com/kids/
Mysteries to solve, scary stories, magic tricks and contests.

Kids Online
http://www.kidsonline.co.uk/
A general entertainment site for children.

TV

Most children's television programmes now have websites which provide games and information.

CBBC
http://www.bbc.co.uk/cbbc/
Children's BBC links to all children's television programmes on the BBC.

Blue Peter
http://www.bbc.co.uk/bluepeter/

CITV
http://www.itv.co.uk/citv.htm
Children's ITV.

Cartoon Network
http://www.cartoonnetwork.co.uk/

Nickelodeon
http://www.nicktv.co.uk/

MTV
http://www.mtv.co.uk/

Computer games

Girl Tech
http://www.girltech.com/
For the female computer enthusiast.

Games Domain
http://www.gamesdomain.co.uk/
All things computer-game related, including reviews, patches and walk-throughs.

Games Domain Review
http://www.gamesdomain.co.uk/gdreview/
An online independent magazine about computer games.

Gamespot UK
http://www.gamespot.co.uk/
More computer games material.

Seussville Games
http://www.randomhouse.com/seussville/games/
Online games with a Seussville theme.

Music/pop

Yahooligans List of Musicians and Pop Stars
http://www.yahooligans.com/Arts_and_Entertainment/Music/Musicians/

Films

Disney

http://www.disney.co.uk/

Games, information and lots of general Disney material.

Yahooligans – Movies – Titles

http://www.yahooligans.com/Arts_and_Entertainment/Movies/Titles/

A collection of links to specific movie sites, eg *Star Wars*.

The Internet Movie Database for Kids

http://kids.imdb.com/

Film facts and figures for kids.

Sport

Carling Net

http://www.fa-premier.com/

The official website of the Carling Football Premiership.

Manchester United

http://www.manutd.com/

Official website of the ubiquitous club.

Netball Resources Page

http://www.ucl.ac.uk/~uczcw11/netball.htm

Collection of links to all things netball related.

International Gymnast Kids' Club

http://www.intlgymnast.com/kidsklub/

UK Athletics

http://www.ukathletics.org/

Information for librarians and parents

Although there are many excellent resources on the Internet, there is also some dubious material. The following resource will teach parents about the dangers that exist for their children on the Internet and how these dangers can be avoided. All libraries should ensure that their child users of the Internet have undergone some kind of *SafeSurfing* training.

SafeSurfin'

http://www.safesurfin.com/

Essential information about how kids can surf safely and the rules that they should follow while online.

9
Community information resources

- ★ Advice and support
- ★ Community networks

The term 'community information' can be difficult to define precisely, although it is one familiar in public libraries. The term is perhaps most usefully defined by the kinds of information that such a collection contains. Typically, a public library's collection contains material on local events, activities, educational opportunities perhaps, and social and welfare information, for example. Some of these categories will overlap with those described in other chapters in this part of the book, such as government information and learning and education.

As well as the Internet being used in the provision of information, communities themselves are harnessing the interactive potential of the new information and communications technologies to create community information networks. These networks allow communities to join together to share in common interests and concerns.

Local authority websites are likely to provide a good deal of community information; addresses for these sites can be found in Chapter 12. In this chapter we highlight UK national sites that are providing advice and support services as well as links to specific community networks.

Advice and support

National Association of Citizens Advice Bureaux
http://www.nacab.org.uk/
Provides basic information and advice online about many areas commonly of interest such as employment rights, housing and civil rights. Full text of CAB policy documents is also available. The site provides details of the services

available in local CAB offices. Some bureaux offer advice by e-mail and some have their own websites.

Age Concern
http://www.ace.org.uk/
Advice and information from the charity concerned with the welfare of older people.

Lawlinks
http://library.ukc.ac.uk/library/lawlinks/
An annotated list of UK, European and international legal information on the Internet, provided by the University of Kent Law School. The resource includes sections on UK legislation, international human rights and student resources.

Useful information on UK Charities
http://pitch.phon.ucl.ac.uk/home/dave/TOC_H/Charities/
A simple A–Z listing of UK charities with a presence on the Internet and other related resources. Includes a link to US and German charities.

Environment Agency: Your Environment
http://www.environment-agency.gov.uk/your_env/
An English and Welsh government agency delivering information on the environment. The website encourages involvement in initiatives to improve the quality of air, land and water. The Your Backyard feature of this site allows you to access environmental data, such as the quality of bathing waters and pollution in areas identified by postcode.

Disability Net
http://www.disabilitynet.co.uk/
Provides disability information and news. Includes links to UK government and non-governmental related agencies and job vacancies, and provides a discussion area. Primarily UK-focused.

National Lottery Good Causes
http://www.national-lottery.co.uk/causes/
Here you can find out about the sorts of projects that are eligible to bid for lottery money. A database gives information about all projects that have previously been awarded funds.

Contact a Family

http://www.cafamily.org.uk/

Contact a Family is a charity helping families who care for children with any disability or special need. There is a directory of rare syndromes, with contact details of support groups and online factsheets for carers. The charity also promotes self-help by putting families in touch with other families in similar situations and helping parents to develop their own local or national support groups.

The Samaritans

http://www.samaritans.org.uk/

This site includes reports and information produced by the organization. You can contact a counsellor by e-mail. A confidential service allows you to send e-mails without your address being disclosed to the receiver.

Community networks

Gateway to Community Information

http://www.slainte.org.uk/comminfo/commhome.htm

This gateway to community information has been designed by the Scottish EARL Community Information Taskgroup for library staff, but would be of use to all users. All sites have been assessed for quality and relevance. The site is obviously heavy on Scottish resources, but there is much of general use and interest.

UK Communities Online

http://www.communities.org.uk/

Communities Online aims to address issues of sustainability, social inclusion and healthier economies by focusing on the use of new communications technologies in localities. The site has lots of information about what community networking is and how such networks are developing. The site will be of use to those wanting to develop community networks as well as just find out more about the topic through e-mail discussion lists and the resources available.

UK Community Networks

http://panizzi.shef.ac.uk/community/uk.htm

A useful A–Z list of some of the community networks that are up and running. Sites will vary in the information and services that they offer, but typically include information on local sports and social clubs, travel information, educational opportunities, etc.

10

Consumer information resources

- ★ General resources
- ★ Consumer associations
- ★ National government bodies
- ★ Industry Ombudsmen and regulators
- ★ Financial advice
- ★ Homes
- ★ Law
- ★ Cars
- ★ Holidays
- ★ Buying on the net

UK consumer information is easily found on the Internet. Official bodies such as the Office of Fair Trading and the Citizens Advice Bureaux have published many of their advice leaflets online, and collections of consumer information links make it easy to identify relevant organizations for help. Specialized bodies such as the Industry Ombudsmen are also online, making them as available to the individual as they are to the local Trading Standards Officer.

Information about health and travel will be found in Chapters 13 and 20.

General resources

The five sites listed below are excellent starting-points for finding consumer information on the Internet. They are a mixture of actual collections of advice and guides to where to find relevant resources on the Internet.

Trading Standards Net

http://www.tradingstandards.net/

Packed full of extremely useful content, *Trading Standards Net* is a good first stop in the search for consumer information. It includes a message-board where people can post their consumer problems, a mailing list and a large collection of useful links. The site is maintained by a Trading Standards Officer and has regular updates.

Watchdog

http://www.bbc.co.uk/watchdog/

The popular BBC programme has an extensive website which is packed with useful resources. Information about cases featured in the programme is provided, as well as guides about how to buy a car, how to buy a house, how to go to court and so on. There is also a very useful collection of consumer information links.

Trading Standards Central

http://www.tradingstandards.gov.uk/

A one-stop shop for consumer protection information in the UK. The site is supported and maintained by ITSA, the Institute of Trading Standards Administration. It includes online leaflets and information about recently recalled products.

National Association of Citizens Advice Bureaux

http://www.nacab.org.uk/

Information about NACAB, where you can find your local CAB and national policy issues on which they are currently advising government.

Advice Guide

http://www.adviceguide.org.uk/

This is the online advice service provided by NACAB. Information and advice is available on a wide range of topics and the site provides information for England, Wales and Scotland. The range of topics covered is very extensive and can be keyword searched or browsed by topic or alphabetical order.

Consumer associations

Most of the consumer associations in the UK have websites. The range of information available on these sites varies.

Which Online
http://www.which.net/

Which Online is the website of the Consumer Association and is a charged service. Some of the content of the site is available for free, but this is only a very small proportion of the 50,000 pages of information that it provides.

Welsh Consumer Association
http://www.consumerinformation.wales.org/

General Consumer Council for Northern Ireland
http://www.nics.gov.uk/gcc/

Scottish Consumer Council
http://www.connections.gcal.ac.uk/scotconsumer/

National government bodies

The Northern Ireland Trading Standards Service
http://www.tssni.gov.uk/

The Office of Fair Trading
http://www.oft.gov.uk/

Industry Ombudsmen and regulators

Local Government Ombudsmen
http://www.open.gov.uk/lgo/

Local Government Ombudsmen investigate complaints about most council matters including housing, planning, education, social services, consumer protection, drainage and council tax. The Ombudsmen can also investigate complaints about a council's methods.

Northern Ireland Ombudsmen
http://ombudsman.nics.gov.uk/

They cover Parliamentary, local government and health complaints.

OFTEL
http://www.oftel.gov.uk/

The telecommunications regulator.

OFGEM
http://www.ofgem.gov.uk/
The electricity and gas market regulator.

OFWAT
http://www.open.gov.uk/ofwat/index.htm
The water industry regulator.

The Insurance Ombudsman
http://www.theiob.org.uk/
This site provides very limited information about how to make a complaint or get advice, but does provide lots of examples of cases submitted to them and how they were resolved.

Office of the Banking Ombudsman
http://www.obo.org.uk/
Information about how to make a complaint to your bank.

Financial advice

Information about the finance industries is readily available on the Internet. Most of the major financial advice organizations and their regulators have websites.

Council of Mortgage Lenders
http://www.cml.org.uk/
Information about the Mortgage Code and useful FAQs about buying a house, how to make complaints about your mortgage and how mortgage lenders handle arrears and repossessions.

Association of British Insurers: Consumer Information
http://www.abi.org.uk/consumer2/consumer.htm
ABI has produced a range of information sheets full of useful advice to consumers on a number of insurance issues. Subjects include motor, household, travel, medical and life insurance and pensions.

Finance Industry Standards Association
http://www.fisa.co.uk/
A website that is still limited, but does provide information about FISA's code of standards.

Financial Services Authority
http://www.fsa.gov.uk/
Contains information about how to make complaints against a financial advisor and how to claim compensation. Also includes the Central Register, a database of firms currently authorized to carry on investment business in the UK. The database is free for the private individual to use, but you must complete an online registration form.

Moneyworld
http://www.moneyworld.co.uk/
A personal finance website which provides guides on buying a house, pensions, insurance and investments. Also has a best-buy mortgage database which searches 1400 products against your mortgage needs profile.

MoneyWeb
http://www.moneyweb.co.uk/
Lots of good basic information on all matters concerning pensions, mortgages, investments, life insurance, etc. Also valuable information for industry professionals, looking at compliance on the Internet and other issues.

Investment Management Regulatory Organisation Ltd (IMRO)
http://www.imro.co.uk/

Motley Fool
http://www.fool.co.uk
A personal finance site to accompany the successful Motley Fool series of books.

Homes

Many of the national organizations dealing with house-building, selling and maintenance have websites. The ones listed below are some of the major ones. There are also a considerable number of commercial websites which list houses for sale across the country and give general advice about buying, selling and maintaining houses. These types of sites can easily be found by using any major search engine.

National House-Building Council (NHBC)
http://www.nhbc.co.uk/
Information about what to look for when you're buying a new house and how

to make complaints. It also provides a database of builders registered with the NHBC.

National Association of Estate Agents
http://www.naea.co.uk/
Information about how to make complaints about estate agents, top tips on how to make your house as saleable as possible and access to *Property Live* – a database of properties for sale around the UK.

National Federation of Builders
http://www.builders.org.uk/
At the time of writing this site was very limited in scope.

Institute of Plumbers
http://www.plumbers.org.uk/
Includes a free database of all their members searchable by postcode.

Law

Initially many legal organizations were slow to take advantage of the Internet, but this is now rapidly changing. The organizations listed in this section are examples of the type of information that is now available. The Advice Centre site of the Citizens Advice Bureaux listed under 'General resources' also provides much legal advice.

The Law Society
http://www.lawsoc.org.uk/
Provides advice and guidance on how to find a solicitor and at the time of writing was in the process of making a directory of qualified solicitors available online.

Legal Aid Board (England and Wales)
http://www.legal-aid.gov.uk

Scottish Legal Aid Board
http://www.slab.org.uk/

LawRights
http://www.lawrights.co.uk/
LawRights provides free legal information for England and Wales. Information is divided into FAQ's and fact sheets on a wide range of topics.

Cars

Cars are one of the topics which cause most consumer complaints. Many car magazines provide access to their reviews on their sites and organizations like the Retail Motor Industry Federation provide guidelines and advice about how to buy a car. The Office of Fair Trading also has a large section on its site about buying cars. Other useful resources may be newsgroups about cars.

Retail Motor Industry Federation
http://www.rmif.co.uk/

What Car?
http://www.whatcar.co.uk/
The online version of the car review magazine which includes its road test reviews library. There is also an option for an assisted search to identify the type of car which most perfectly matches your needs.

Buying A Car: Office of Fair Trading
http://www.oft.gov.uk/html/cars/home.htm
Advice from the OFT about how to go about buying a car, what to look for and what to do if things go wrong.

Carbusters – European Car Buying
http://www.carbusters.com/
The Consumer Association's guide to buying a car more cheaply in mainland Europe.

Holidays

More information on holiday resources is available in Chapter 20.

Association of British Travel Agents (ABTA)
http://www.abtanet.com/

Timeshare Consumers Association
http://www.timeshare.org.uk/
Provides information about the latest timeshare scams to be aware of.

Buying on the Net

It is now possible to buy many products and services over the Internet. The Office of Fair Trading offers advice about the best way to purchase online and what your rights are. The Consumers Association provides a list of web traders who satisfy their code of practice – though this list is limited at present. There are also a number of other organizations or businesses who aim to provide impartial guidance about online services and businesses and the products offered.

Online Shopping Advice from the OFT
http://www.oft.gov.uk/html/shopping/
Tips about buying things online from the Office of Fair Trading.

The Which? Consumer Association Web Trader Scheme
http://www.which.net/webtrader/

Active Buyer's Guide
http://www.activebuyersguide.com/
Active Buyer takes you through a number of question and answers about the sort of appliance that you want to buy, how much you want to pay and what facilities are most important to you. At the end of these questions it provides you with a list of models which most closely match your needs. It claims to be unbiased and independent and therefore seems to be a useful resource. Again this is a US-based service: prices are in dollars and some recommendations may be models which are not available in the UK. However if you're after something mainstream you may be lucky.

BizRate.com
http://www.bizrate.com/
BizRate.com claims to give online shoppers a trustworthy, completely unbiased web resource to use when making important online buying decisions. It reviews online commercial services and businesses and provides a search engine so you can compare the cost of items in one go between these businesses. At the moment the focus is on US-based businesses.

ValueMed
http://www.valuemed.co.uk
ValueMed searches across a number of different e-retailers and tells you where you can buy something for the least money. This service is provided by Asda.

11

Family and local history resources

- ★ General resources
- ★ UK national record offices
- ★ International archives and record offices
- ★ Local record offices and archives
- ★ Online databases
- ★ Mailing lists and discussion lists
- ★ Family history societies
- ★ Local history organizations
- ★ Local history photograph collections
- ★ Local history publications

Family and local history are some of the fastest growing types of resources on the Internet. Genealogists and local history researchers have until recently had to be willing to travel to many geographically disparate locations to search by hand through local collections. The increasing availability of family and local history material on the Internet has meant that this material is now at a PC near you. As well as resources being more easily available, the use of e-mail and discussion lists has meant that people with similar research interests have been able to discover each other and share their research. Already many public libraries are receiving e-mails from family and local history enthusiasts from around the world, asking for help with their research.

This chapter points to some of the more useful family and local history resources which are available online. Much source material is still not available electronically, nor are the vast majority of archival catalogues. However, what is available shows the potential that the Internet offers the family and local history researcher. Due to the vast amount of material on this topic which is available, this chapter can only provide a taster of what is out there. Where possible, web directories on specific topics have been included in order to provide the reader with good starting-points for their own searches.

Family history general resources

This section provides a list of excellent starting-points for family history material. These resources are web directories which classify, organize and provide access to many of the 1000s of genealogy resources which are available on the Internet. A selection of UK-focused resources and more international collections have been included.

Familia
http://www.earl.org.uk/familia/
Familia is a web-based directory of family history resources held in public libraries in the UK and Ireland. Updated and maintained by the Family History Group of the EARL Consortium it is the online starting place to find information about family history materials in public libraries in the UK.

The UK & Ireland Genealogical Information Service (GENUKI)
http://www.genuki.org.uk/
The aim of *GENUKI* is to serve as a 'virtual reference library' of genealogical information that is of particular relevance to the UK and Ireland. It is a non-commercial service, provided by an ever-growing group of volunteers in cooperation with the Federation of Family History Societies and a number of its member societies. Not the most visually attractive site, it is however of great importance and is probably the most comprehensive site available about UK genealogy.

Cyndi's List of Genealogy Sites on the Internet
http://www.cyndislist.com/
This is a huge compilation of genealogy Internet resources. It contains over 53,000 links organized into over 100 categories.

UK national record offices and other national organizations

National record offices are the repositories of the national archives. They bring together the records of the government and courts of law and make them available to anyone. These records, including birth certificates, wedding certificates and census material, make them extremely useful for the genealogist.

Public Record Office

http://www.pro.gov.uk/

The Public Record Office is the national repository of archives for England and Wales. In 1999 it launched an Internet-accessible version of its 8-million item catalogue of document descriptions (**http://www.pro.gov.uk/finding/default.htm**). Currently very little of the Record Office's source material is available in electronic format over the Internet. Some particularly famous documents are available in digital format in the Record Office's *Learning Curve* site (**http://www.pro.gov.uk/learningcurve/**), which has been designed for use in schools. Usefully the Record Office has published on its website many of its leaflets about how to undertake genealogy research, and how to use the Record Office.

Public Record Office of Northern Ireland

http://proni.nics.gov.uk/

The Public Record Office of Northern Ireland (PRONI) provides similar types of information to the Public Record Office. General information is provided about how to use PRONI, the type of records that it holds and opening hours information. PRONI's catalogue is not yet available online.

Scottish Record Office

http://www.sro.gov.uk/

At the time of writing this site was empty except for a 'coming soon' message. The address has been included, however, in the hope that the site will have gone live by the time this book is published. The National Archives of Scotland website (**http://www.nas.gov.uk/**) is also under development at the time of writing.

Royal Commission on Historical Manuscripts

http://www.hmc.gov.uk/main.htm

ARCHON

http://www.hmc.gov.uk/archon/archon.htm

ARCHON is the principal information gateway for UK archivists and users of manuscript sources for British history. It is hosted and maintained by the Royal Commission on Historical Manuscripts. From here you can access information on all repositories in the UK and all those repositories throughout the world which have collections of manuscripts which are noted on the British National Register of Archives. In addition, archivists can access information on archival organizations and initiatives through the pages of archivists' links.

International archives and record offices

A large percentage of national archives around the world have websites. Again, these websites range greatly in the type of information and material which they make available online. Some of the more developed online archives are listed below. Also listed is a web directory to national archives on the Internet.

National Archives of New Zealand
http://www.archives.dia.govt.nz/

National Archives of Australia
http://www.naa.gov.au/

National Archives of Canada
http://www.archives.ca/

National Archives and Records Administration of USA
http://www.nara.gov/

Archivesinfo, overseas archival repositories on the Internet
http://www.archivesinfo.net/overseas.html

Local record offices and archives

Local record offices and archives in the UK are also beginning to develop websites. The range of information and the quality of the sites vary greatly. Many provide little more than information about their opening times and location. Others, for example the Suffolk Record Office, will have lists of their recent accessions, online exhibitions and information about their collections and how to use them. The Somerset Record Office has detailed information about parishes and digitized parish maps from 1900, in addition to digitized postcards.

UK Public Libraries Page
http://dspace.dial.pipex.com/town/square/ac940/ukpublib.html
The *UK Public Libraries Page* is an online directory for public library web pages. Record offices and archives are often part of the local library service and so this directory will be helpful in locating them.

Archivesinfo, UK Archival Repositories on the Internet
http://www.archivesinfo.net/uksites.html
A good collection of links to UK local record offices.

Suffolk Record Office
http://www.suffolkcc.gov.uk/libraries_and_heritage/sro/

Somerset Archive and Record Service
http://www.somerset.gov.uk/archives/

Online databases

There is a developing genealogy industry on the Internet. Large databases of family history material have been gathered by commercial companies who charge access to them via the web. Most of these sites have a US focus. Although charges are made for much of the content, some of it is free. *Ancestry.com* for instance, provides a free searchable family-tree database which is the largest collection of family trees on the Internet. The largest genealogy database which is available on the Internet, however, is free and is provided by The Church of Jesus Christ of Latter-Day Saints. Other useful databases for family historians can also be the online telephone directories which are increasingly being made available (see Chapter 18).

FamilySearch Internet Genealogy Service
http://www.familysearch.org/
The FamilySearch® Internet Genealogy Service gives you access to extensive genealogical resources gathered by The Church of Jesus Christ of Latter-Day Saints. This service includes free access to the International Genealogy Index, the world's largest collection of birth, christening, and marriage information with over 300 million records.

Family Name Archive Library
http://www.traceit.com/
Seven databases available online with one million surnames referenced.

Commonwealth War Graves Commission
http://yard.ccta.gov.uk/cwgc/register.nsf
This register provides personal and service details and places of commemoration for the 1.7 million members of the Commonwealth forces who died in World War One or Two.

Ancestry.com
http://www.ancestry.com/
A commercial genealogy company.

The RootsWeb
http://www.rootsweb.com/
A semi-commercial genealogy site.

Mailing lists and discussion lists

There are numerous mailing lists and discussion lists which are on the topic of genealogy and genealogical research. The two addresses below are of directories which list a considerable number of these.

Genealogy on the Internet
http://www.rootsweb/~jfuller/gen_mail.html

Genealogy on the Internet – Newsgroups
http://www.genhomepage.com/communications.html

Family history societies

Family history societies are also developing their own resources and are always useful contacts for help and sharing research.

Federation of Family History Member Societies
http://www.ffhs.org.uk/members/
An extensive list of family history societies on the web.

Society of Genealogists
http://www.sog.org.uk/
Information about the UK Society of Genealogists.

Local history general resources

Many of the resources that are relevant for family historians are also relevant for local historians; however, this section is specifically focused on local history resources. Again, the Internet has proved to be a boon to the local historian. It is very easy to publish research, search catalogues remotely and to locate people who share the same interests.

Historical Text Archive
http://www.geocities.com/Athens/Forum/9061/

Visually unappealing, but a vast collection of links about history resources on the Internet.

Local history organizations

Royal Commission on Historical Monuments of England (RCHME)
http://www.rchme.gov.uk/homepage.html

The RCHME is a national body which has responsibility for creating and maintaining a public record of England's historical buildings and archeological landscapes. As part of its work it has developed the National Monuments Record which is a public archive of data on the historic environment, open to all and free of charge. It now comprises over 12 million photographs, drawings, maps and records, a substantial reference library of published books and journals, and several indexes of other related material. The RCHME is planning to make the catalogue for this archive available online at some time in the future.

Royal Commission on the Ancient and Historical Monuments of Scotland (RCAHMS)
http://www.rcahms.gov.uk/

The RCAHMS website provides access to Canmore – Computer Application for National MOnument Record Enquiries. Canmore is the catalogue of RCAHMS and while not providing access to digitized images themselves, it does provide textual information about them. You need to complete an online registration form to use this catalogue but registration is free.

Institute for Historical Research
http://www.ihr.sas.ac.uk/

Contains *History Online* which has a searchable catalogue of 30,000 history resource records.

BBC Education History Resources
http://www.bbc.co.uk/history/

Lots of general information about history available on the BBC website. Specific resources do relate to some community history, for example the Windrush resources. Also included is information about Radio Four's 'Making History' programme (**http://www.bbc.co.uk/history/programmes/makinghistory/millenium. shtml**).

Local history photograph collections

Some public libraries and archives have already digitized some of their local photograph collections and made them available on the Internet. The extent of the collection which has been digitized varies greatly, but resources like these have proved to be very popular and successful.

Cambridgeshire's History on the Internet
http://www.camcnty.gov.uk/library/history/home1.htm

Leeds Library and Information Services Photograph Collection
http://www.leeds.gov.uk/archive/

Local history publications

Local History Magazine
http://www.local-history.co.uk/
The website of the UK's only dedicated local history magazine. This site contains a useful collection of local history links, information about local history courses taking place around the country and contact details for local history societies in the UK.

Victoria History of the Counties of England
http://ihr.sas.ac.uk/vch/
Information provided on this site includes work in progress and volumes published. More detailed information is provided about the *Victoria County History of Wiltshire* at: **http://www.ihrinfo.ac.uk/vch/wilts/wilts.html.**

Internet Library of Early Journals
http://www.bodley.ox.ac.uk/ilej/
The Internet Library of Early Journals is a joint project by the Universities of Birmingham, Leeds, Manchester and Oxford, conducted under the auspices of the Electronic Libraries Programme. It aims to digitize substantial runs of 18th- and 19th-century journals, and make these images available on the Internet, together with their associated bibliographic data. Journals used in the project include *Gentleman's Magazine*, *The Annual Register*, *Philosophical Transactions of the Royal Society*, *Notes and Queries*, *The Builder* and *Blackwood's Edinburgh Magazine.*

History Today
http://www.historytoday.com/

The online version of this monthly history magazine. Contains a searchable index of the magazine since 1990 with many of the articles available free online. Also contains a useful set of history links.

12

Government resources

- ★ National UK government
- ★ Local UK government
- ★ Europe
- ★ International government
- ★ General resources

Governments and official organizations have seized upon the Internet as a means of delivering better and more convenient services to citizens as the much-heralded 'Information Society' evolves. A number of UK government initiatives in, for example, the health and welfare services have placed electronic communications at the heart of plans to widen participation to the democratic society. The Internet is seen not only as a way of providing one-way information, but increasingly as a way of governments and official bodies interacting with their electorate. Increasingly you will find online ways of communicating with these bodies. The potential to reduce paperwork and trips to post, tax and other government offices is substantial and in the UK, the Government have stated that 25% of government services will be accessible electronically by 2002. A number of MPs now have e-mail addresses and some have their own web pages providing local information on their constituencies.

National UK government

open.gov.uk
http://www.open.gov.uk/

A starting-point to the Government's information service. Here you will find links to all government departments and offices. This gateway will point you in the right direction for what you need.

UK Statutory Instruments
http://www.hmso.gov.uk/stat.htm
All statutory instruments since 1997 are available here in full text.

House of Lords
http://www.parliament.the-stationery-office.co.uk/pa/id/idhome.htm
Information about the House of Lords including full text of all judgments since Novembert 1996.

Department for Culture, Media and Sport
http://www.culture.gov.uk/
Primarily provides information about the work of the department. The site hosts the National Lottery Awards website, which includes a searchable database of lottery awards.

Number 10
http://www.number-10.gov.uk/
The section on government press releases is updated daily. You can post your comments on aspects of government to the open discussion e-mail list and listen to live prime ministerial broadcasts. Also includes a history of Number 10 Downing Street, and brief biographies of recent prime ministers.

United Kingdom Parliament
http://www.parliament.the-stationery-office.co.uk/
Entry-point for information about the UK Parliament. From here you can search the parliamentary publications database that contains all types of published articles, including Hansard, MPs' written answers and the Register of Members' Interests. The site also includes a list of all members of Parliament with their e-mail addresses and links to websites where available.

UK Government Departments
http://www.soton.ac.uk/~bopcas/centgovt.htm
An A–Z listing of departments. Useful if you know the department you are looking for.

UK Official Publications on the Internet
http://www.official-documents.co.uk/
This Stationery Office site provides full text or summaries of selected official government documents.

BOPCRIS (British Official Publications Collaborative Reader Information Service)
http://www.bopcris.ac.uk
Provides bibliographical details and abstracts of official British publications.

Local UK government

Information available on local authority sites will vary from authority to authority, although from most sites you will be able to find names and contact details (and sometimes e-mail addresses) for elected members, details of council policies and initiatives and links and information for tourists and businesses in the region.

Directory of UK Local Government on the Web
http://www.tagish.co.uk/tagish/links/localgov.htm
Links to all county, metropolitan, unitary, borough and district authority sites. A listing of town and parish council sites is also available here. Tagish is an Information Society consultancy firm and does a lot of work in the public sector. The Essential List on this website is a useful link to UK and worldwide government and public sector-related sites.

Local Government Association
http://www.lga.gov.uk/
Provides information on issues that affect the functioning of local government, such as parliamentary documents and information on the workings of the LGA itself. The Councillors Gateway provides information for elected members. Part of the site is restricted to LGA members only.

BBC's UK Politics site
http://news.bbc.co.uk/hi/english/uk_politics/
As well as the latest UK political news, this large site publishes transcripts of politicians interviewed for the website and there are short biographies about all MPs and SMPs and members of the Welsh Assembly. There is an A–Z of Parliament which explains, for example, the job of the speaker, and the different Parliamentary Bills. Sound and video from the House of Commons, House of Lords, Parliamentary Committees, European Parliament and BBC political programmes are available. The site includes links to all the main UK political parties and a diary of future UK political events.

Europe

The Internet is particularly useful for providing access to the ever-increasing amount of information produced relating to the European Union. Even the smallest branch or mobile library can provide access to the vast amount of documentation available online. Given the amount available, navigation and finding what you want is not particularly easy; *Europa* and *Euroguide* are good places to start though.

Europa
http://europa.eu.int/
Main entry-point to information on and about the European Union. The ABC to the European Union is particularly useful in providing basic information on the EU, citizens' rights and key issues such as the Euro and employment, as well as access to official documents, legal texts, publications and databases, and sources of information. The site is available in 11 European languages.

Euroguide
http://www.euroguide.org/
A subject gateway to the European Union developed by Essex County Libraries and EARL. Resources are found via lists of categories, such as education, libraries, telecommunications, or via an A–Z listing of resources. You can ask questions about the European Union via e-mail and can suggest sites for inclusion in the guide.

Council of Europe
http://www.coe.fr/
Includes a useful presentation explaining what the council is and what it does, as well as all the expected links to council documents, news and related sites. Information is available in French and English.

Governments Online
http://europa.eu.int/abc/governments/index_en.html
Links to citizen-oriented information in European countries. Part of the large *Europa* site.

European Voice Online
http://www.european-voice.com/
The online version of a weekly print newspaper covering European Union affairs.

International government

As well as providing information about a nation's governance, some of these sites, such as *Welcome to the White House*, are useful as a demonstration of the potential ways in which governments can exploit the interactivity of the Internet to make themselves more accountable to their citizens.

Websites on National Parliaments
http://www.polisci.umn.edu/information/parliaments/index.html
A simple A–Z list of parliamentary sites provided by the Department of Political Science at the University of Minnesota. Other resources available on the site, such as US governmental and political sites, may also be of interest.

Politicians around the world
http://www.trytel.com/~aberdeen/
Names and (postal) addresses of monarchs, presidents, prime ministers and governors in 195 countries. E-mail addresses and web pages are becoming available. A great resource, if it continues to be kept up to date. Also containing links to resources on lobbying.

World-Wide Web Virtual Library: US Government Information Sources
http://www.nttc.edu/gov_res.html
A useful starting-point to all aspects of US government.

Welcome to the White House
http://www.whitehouse.gov/
The site aims to improve the ways in which the US government uses the Internet to communicate with its citizens. Access is available to all online resources made available by US government agencies via a subject index and a free-text search engine. E-mails can be sent to the President, Vice-President and their spouses. A history of the White House and its occupants is available and you can listen to (and read the transcript of) the President's weekly radio addresses. The White House for Kids shows the White House from a child's perspective.

The Commonwealth Online
http://www.tcol.co.uk/
This is the official site of the Commonwealth and provides much information about the organization itself. The Member Countries section provides useful summaries of aspects such as transportation, and economic, legal, constitutional and geographic facts.

FedWorld
http://www.fedworld.gov/
A useful starting-point of searching out US Government information.

General resources

For the academic and general enquiry.

Internet Resource Guides from Keele University Department of Politics
http://www.psr.keele.ac.uk/
A list of useful resources from the University of Keele. Covers governmental and political resources in a number of countries and includes constitutions, treaties, declarations, manifestos and political philosophy. The data archives provide links to a wide range of sources of statistics.

SOSIG: Politics
http://www.sosig.ac.uk/politics/
Politics section of the Social Science Information Gateway. Provides quality-assured Internet resources.

13

Health resources

- ★ General resources
- ★ Condition-specific sites
- ★ Public health
- ★ Reference resources
- ★ Medical gateways

As more emphasis is placed on greater personal responsibility for health and welfare issues, the Internet affords even the smallest of libraries the ability to provide access to a vast amount of health-related resources on even the most rare and uncommon health conditions. In addition to the quantity of resources available, library users may value the privacy and relative anonymity of searching the Internet for information on sensitive, personal matters, compared with asking library staff for help in finding material or initiating interlibrary loans. Patients and their carers can find support from the many virtual self-help groups that exist online. Such groups can be particularly valuable in cases of rarer conditions where local support groups would not exist.

The accuracy of information on this subject is vital and, for this reason, many of the sites suggested are from widely known reputable authorities. Often, less 'authoritative' providers will publish a disclaimer on the site stating that the information is provided for educational purposes only and should not be seen as a substitute for expert advice by a qualified health professional.

General resources

Department of Health
http://www.doh.gov.uk/

Government information and links to related sites. The department is develop-ng *Wired for Health*, a web initiative to provide health information for children and their teachers.

Health Education Authority
http://www.hea.org.uk/heamenu.html

Health resources, advice and information about the campaigning and research activities of the organization. The multimedia section includes *QUICK*, the quality information checklist, which has been designed to help children assess the quality of the information they find on the Internet. Although many of the examples used are health related, the concepts can be used with any subject, which makes *QUICK* a very useful resource in itself.

British Medical Journal
http://www.bmj.com/

Free access to the full text of all articles published in the weekly *BMJ* from January 1995. The site also contains material which is unique to the website. Letters and responses to articles are published on the site.

Trawling the Net
http://www.shef.ac.uk/~scharr/ir/trawling.html

A wide-ranging list of free databases available on the Internet of interest to UK medical staff, provided by the University of Sheffield.

National Electronic Library for Health
http://www.nelh.nhs.uk/

Although at the time of writing this site is still under construction, the aims are to 'provide easy access to best current knowledge and to improve health and healthcare, clinical practice and patient choice'. The site is intended to be a major factor in the UK Government's initiative for improving the nation's health. The site is currently providing background information on the initiative and an outline of the services that will be available in due course.

NHS Direct Online
http://www.nhsdirect.nhs.uk/

NHS Direct Online is intended as a gateway to high quality, authoritative health information for patients. The site provides access to evaluated resources from external sources on a range of conditions and healthy living, as well as information about the nurse-led NHS Direct telephone service which will eventually be developed online as well.

Condition-specific sites

As well as general sites, many other resources will aim to provide information and advice on specific conditions. Many of the sites aimed at providing support and advice for patients and their carers will include mailing lists and e-mail discussion groups. Resources on some of the more common conditions have been included as examples below. Information on rarer conditions can be found using some of the gateways and indexes listed here, as well as through general Internet search engines. Support groups for these conditions can be particularly valuable as patients and their carers may be spread over a wide geographic area, making physical contact extremely difficult.

Royal National Institute for the Blind
http://www.rnib.org.uk/
Provides information for the visually impaired and for professionals working in the field of vision impairment as well as information on the campaigning activities of the RNIB. Includes an e-mail discussion forum. The home page contains some useful tips on ways you can alter the settings on your web browser if you are having difficulty viewing websites. The site is approved by Bobby, a web tool that analyses sites for their accessibility to people with disabilities.

British Diabetic Association
http://www.diabetes.org.uk/
Provides information for living with diabetes and details of the research programmes that the organization is involved in. An area is dedicated to supporting teenagers with the condition.

Cancerhelp UK
http://medweb.bham.ac.uk/cancerhelp/
Information service about cancer and cancer care, designed for general use by the Medical School at the University of Birmingham. It provides information on a range of related topics including cancer prevention, diagnosis, treatment and follow-up and has a glossary of common terms and a questions and answers section for adults. A section for children is currently been developed. Meanwhile some links are provided to other sites aimed specifically at children.

AMA Health Insight
http://www.ama-assn.org/consumer.htm
The consumer section of the large American Medical Association site. Inform-

ation on specific conditions, family and general health issues are easily found from drop-down menus. The Interactive Health section provides quick and simple to use personal assessments on health and fitness. The Human Atlas, available from the General Health section, provides simple diagrams of the major structures of the human body.

Internet Mental Health
http://www.mentalhealth.com/

A free encyclopaedia of mental health information. Includes online diagnostic programs that can be used to diagnose anxiety disorders, eating disorders, mood disorders, personality disorders and substance-related disorders. It is made clear that these are intended as an aid to diagnosis only and not as a substitute for expert advice by qualified health professionals.

Alzheimer's Disease Society
http://www.alzheimers.org.uk/

Information and support primarily aimed at carers, from the UK care and research charity for people with dementia.

CancerWeb
http://www.graylab.ac.uk/cancerweb.html

A UK-based information resource which is organized according to type of user, e whether you are looking at the site as a patient, a clinician or researcher.

Interconnections
http://www.interconnections.co.uk/

The Health section of this site provides information on a range of complementary and natural health therapies. Messages can be posted to the site and an online live chat forum has just been introduced.

Public health

Healthnet
http://www.healthnet.org.uk/

A health promotion site from the Coronary Prevention Groups. Provides facts on healthy lifestyles and links to healthy living magazines and news items.

World Health Organization
http://www.who.int/

Contains reports about the work of the World Health Organization, its policies and a wide range of health-related statistical information as well as detailed information about diseases and health issues.

Reference resources

The On-line Medical Dictionary
http://www.graylab.ac.uk/omd/
Contains terms relating to anything to do with medicine or science. It is produced by the *CancerWeb* project.

Go Ask Alice!
http://www.goaskalice.columbia.edu/
Go Ask Alice! is a health question and answer site produced by Alice!, Columbia University's Health Education Program. Alice will answer questions about physical, sexual, emotional and spiritual health. You can also search the *Go Ask Alice!* archives containing over 1500 previously posted questions and answers.

Drug InfoNet
http://www.druginfonet.com/
This is a large US site covering health-related information and news. The drug information, although American, includes information on pharmaceuticals for patients and health professionals provided by the manufacturers.

Committee on Safety of Medicines
http://www.open.gov.uk/mca/
This is the UK government agency responsible for the quality and safety of medicines. The site provides the latest guidelines and advice. A drug safety bulletin, published four times a year, can be found in the Current Problems in Pharmacovigilance section, and contains information about problems with drugs and advice on how they may be used more safely. The site and publications are designed for health professionals, but could be of general use.

RxList - The Internet Drug Index
http://www.rxlist.com/
Although a US site, it contains extensive pharmacological and general usage information about prescriptive drugs and alternative medicines. Links are provided in the texts to a dictionary.

Medical gateways

Medline Plus

http://www.nlm.nih.gov/medlineplus/

A selected list of health-related resources from the US National Library of Medicine. Sites are selected according to a published selection criteria.

MedicineNet

http://www.medicinenet.com/

A US site designed to provide in-depth medical information written by medical professionals to consumers. A comprehensive site that includes medical news, feature articles, information on diseases and conditions, a medical dictionary and a guide to over-the-counter remedies.

Health Index UK

http://www.healthindex.co.uk/

Gateway to UK healthcare sites on the web. The site is designed for all those involved in healthcare including patients and their carers.

Patient UK

http://www.patient.co.uk/

This site provides links to primarily UK resources on many areas of health including travel health, information for carers and UK self-help and patient groups. Includes a listing of many telephone helpline services.

OMNI

http://www.omni.ac.uk/

OMNI is a gateway to Internet resources in medicine-related topics. All resources are evaluated and a critical summary of each resource is provided. Although the service has been designed for higher education, much of the content will be of general use as well.

UK Health Centre

http://www.healthcentre.org.uk/

Links to health-related sites. Includes a section on complementary therapies.

Medisearch

http://www.medisearch.co.uk/

A collection of authoritative UK and international health resources and news stories. The site also provides a roundup of international business, sports and entertainment news.

14

Home computing and Internet resources

- ★ General resources
- ★ Beginners' guides
- ★ Personal computer companies
- ★ Computer reviews
- ★ Software
- ★ UK Internet Service Providers
- ★ Technical help
- ★ Magazines and papers

Unsurprisingly there is a wide range of information about the Internet itsel and home computing available online. As long as you can get connected you'l be able to find someone or something to help make your computer existenc more satisfying.

General resources

CNET.com
http://home.cnet.com/
A general IT website with lots of information about all aspects of computing IT news and links to other relevant resources.

The Virtual Museum of Computing
http://vmoc.i.am
Find out who invented the first computer and how it worked.

Beginners' guides

Learning how to use a personal computer can be a difficult experience and there are a number of online tutorials which have been designed to help people acquire these new skills. The ones listed below are UK resources, but there are also many other international ones – particularly American – available. As always *Yahoo!* is a good starting point for additional information.

Computers

Getting Started at Home – from the BBC's Computers Don't Bite Campaign
http://www.bbc.co.uk/education/cdb/getting/gstarth.shtml

IT for All
http://www.itforall.org.uk/

Internet

There are many beginners' guides to the Internet available. Below is a selection of some of the best and a directory which provides guidance about many more. Introductory courses to the Internet are available both in the form of web pages and also via e-mail.

BBC Webwise Net_Basics
http://www.bbc.co.uk/webwise/basics/

Learn The Net
http://www.learnthenet.com/

Webmonkey Guides
http://hotwired.lycos.com/webmonkey/guides/
Produced by HotWired, these are a series of guides about what the Internet is, how it works and how to make use of it. Helpful information on subjects like how to find a job online and how to plan a trip.

NetLearn: Resources for Learning the Internet
http://www.rgu.ac.uk/~sim/research/netlearn/callist.htm
An award-winning directory of resources on learning about the Internet put together by people at Robert Gordon University.

Personal computer companies

All of the major computer companies have a website – the addresses for some of the most well-known companies are listed below. Information provided on these sites tends to be very promotional, for example lots of information about their products and how to buy them, but often hidden inside the site can be useful FAQs and help guides.

Apple Computer UK
http://www.apple.com/uk/

Compaq
http://www.compaq.co.uk/

Dell
http://www.euro.dell.com/countries/uk/enu/gen/

Hidden within Dell's site is a series of useful FAQs and technical troubleshooting guides.

Gateway
http://www.gw2k.co.uk/

Hewlett Packard
http://www.hp.com/uk/

IBM
http://www-5.ibm.com/uk/

Time
http://www.timecomputers.com/

Tiny
http://www.uk.tiny.com/

Viglen
http://www.viglen.co.uk

Computer reviews

There are many up-to-date and detailed reviews about computer equipment and services on the Internet. Many computer magazines publish reviews on their websites and there are also a number of independent review sites. Typically review sites are primarily aimed at the US market, so expect prices to be in dollars. The sites listed below, however, are all UK-based sites.

IT Reviews
http://www.itreviews.co.uk/
Computer equipment reviews by UK independent professional IT journalists – the reviews available are good, but at the moment this site is still in its infancy and so there is only a limited amount of information available.

Computer Buyer
http://www.comp-buyer.co.uk/
This magazine provides a considerable number of reviews on its website – registration is required but is free. Usefully this is a UK magazine and therefore everything is in pounds sterling.

PCDirect
http://www.zdnet.co.uk/pcdir/reviews/
Another computer magazine which provides free access to its reviews online.

Software

Like computers, software can also be bought, reviewed and accessed for free online. Demos of games, actual products and helplines can all be found. Software comes in roughly three types: standard commercial products, shareware and freeware. When looking for any software it is often useful to start at a software directory site such as the following two:

Topsoft.com
http://topsoft.com/
A useful and extensive searchable directory of shareware, commercial software and freeware.

Versions
http://www.versions.com/
A searchable database of software products – a free e-mail newsletter is also available.

Commercial products

Microsoft is, of course, the most well-known producer of commercial software and there are vast amounts of information about it and its products available on the Internet. There are also considerable amounts of anti-Microsoft resources available too.

Microsoft UK

http://www.microsoft.com/uk/

The UK homepage for the corporation which links to the extensive worldwide home site.

Corel

http://www.corel.com/

Producers of products like WordPerfect and Corel Draw.

Lotus Development Corporation

http://www.lotus.com/

Producer of the Lotus Office suite of software.

Linux

http://www.linux.com

A non-Microsoft operating system, based on UNIX.

Shareware

The term shareware is used to describe a way of marketing software. Instead of having to purchase the software and then install it, shareware allows you to install and try the software first and then decide whether to purchase it. Shareware software tends to be much cheaper than traditional commercial products.

Shareware.com

http://www.shareware.com/

More than 250,000 shareware products available here.

Freeware

Freeware is software which is available for free. That's it.

Freeware Files.com

http://www.freewarefiles.com/

A large searchable directory of freeware.

UK Internet Service Providers

The number of companies who act as Internet Service Providers (ISPs) is ncreasing. Most ISPs provide their users with e-mail addresses, possible web age space and technical help as well as a connection to the Internet. The ome pages of many of these ISPs are designed to act as a starting-point for ccess to the Internet for their subscribers and have useful collections of links which are free for anyone to use.

BTClick
http://btclick.excite.co.uk/

Compuserve
http://www.compuserve.co.uk/

Freeserve
http://www.freeserve.co.uk/

LineOne
http://www.lineone.net/

Microsoft Network
http://msn.co.uk/

Pipex
http://www.pipex.com

WHSmith online
http://www.whsmith.co.uk/

ISPreview
http://ispreview.co.uk
Reviews of ISPs and a directory including most UK ISPs.

Chapter 1 also includes a discussion of ISPs.

Free e-mail

The large number of web-based e-mail services mean that even people without an ISP can have an e-mail address. These services are typically free and involve nothing more than a simple registration form. The e-mail accounts are accessed through a web page and don't require telneting to a specific computer. The main benefit of these accounts is that access to the web means access to your e-mail, irrespective of what ISP the computer is linked to. Many public libraries are finding tourists, people on business trips and students use the library Internet workstations for checking their web-based e-mail.

List of Free E-mail sites at Yahoo!
http://uk.dir.yahoo.com/Business_and_Economy/Companies/Internet_Services/Email_Providers/Free_Email/

Free e-mail services are also discussed in Chapter 3.

Technical help

Free technical support is available in many forms on the Internet. The legions of newsgroups, mailing lists and websites means that someone, somewhere will be able to provide some advice.

What Is
http://whatis.com/
A glossary for all those computing terms – find out exactly what a 'proxy server' is here.

PC Technology Guide
http://www.pctechguide.com/
Explains what all those computer bits do.

PC World Online: Here's How
http://www.pcworld.com/heres_how/
An archive of top tips and help columns from *PC World* – these columns could be more clearly indexed, but provide lots of very useful and free information so it is worth persevering. The site has a search engine and this can be used to help identify the right column. Also available on this useful site are product reviews, free downloads and games information. The magazine is American though, so expect dollars and American manufacturers to be given most prominence.

PC Resources – Newsgroups
http://www.pchelponline.com/resources/55-00-103.htm
A list of newsgroups concerning all things to do with computers – however *uk.comp.misc*, the main UK group, isn't on this list and is worth seeking out.

Deja.com
http://www.deja.com/usenet
Deja.com provides access to thousands of discussion groups and newsgroups, many of which discuss computing and Internet issues.

Magazines and papers

Most IT magazines now have a companion website. Some of these sites provide useful services such as backcopy searches, collections of Internet resources and free downloads.

Lycos Computer Magazines Online

http://www.lycos.co.uk/webguides/computer/m_mags.html

A useful listing of the UK Internet and computer magazines which are available online.

ZDNet UK

http://www.zdnet.co.uk/

A publishing company which specializes in IT magazines. It's developed an extensive website which acts as a gateway to the Internet as well as to its magazines. Its companion US site (**http://www.zdnet.com/**) provides even more computer and Internet-related information and news.

FutureNet: Computing Division

http://www.futurenet.com/futureonline/divisions/computing.asp

Future publish over 25 computer and Internet magazines. This site provides a gateway to their online versions.

15

Illustration resources

- ★ General starting-points
- ★ History and news images
- ★ Sporting images
- ★ Animals and plants images
- ★ Art images
- ★ Architectural images
- ★ Scientific images
- ★ Picture libraries and agencies

There are millions of images available on the Internet. Museums and galleries are making their collections digitally available, artists are developing online exhibitions, commercial companies are selling prints and photo agencies are offering their services online. There is therefore a reasonable chance that somewhere on the Internet there is an illustration of whatever you are after – what makes illustrations on the Internet complicated is the issue of copyright. Just because an image is available to be viewed as part of a website does not mean that it can be legally downloaded and used for something else by the website viewer. There are many sites which state that images are freely available to be used by anyone, but others strictly state that images are copyrighted and can be only be used with permission or for a fee. The best policy to pursue when taking images off the Internet is to ask first. Most websites will have a contact e-mail address and this makes it easy to clarify with the website owner how you may use their images.

General starting-points

When trying to find an image of something, perhaps the easiest and most straightforward way of locating one is simply to search for that topic in a search engine (see page 51). If this doesn't work, it will be time to start using some of the commercial directories that are available. Online picture agencies are good starting-points with some of them having a searchable database of millions of images. These images are typically only freely available for non-commercial personal use and will be clearly marked with the watermark of the company – for non-watermarked images a fee must be paid.

Lycos Images
http://www.lycos.com/picturethis/

Lycos has a database of 80,000 freely available images which range from zebras to Cindy Crawford. Lycos also offers the option of an image-only search of the whole web which contains at least 18 million images. *Lycos Images* is therefore an excellent place to start searching for images. It also provides a similar service for sound clips.

Yahooligans: Download Pictures
http://www.yahooligans.com/Downloader/pictures/

A rare directory of images on the web, organized into categories such as people, sports, holidays. All guaranteed to be child-friendly as *Yahooligans* is aimed at a child audience.

Corbis
http://www.corbis.com/

Corbis makes available 2.1 million images online – ranging from photojournalism to fine art. There is a $3 fee for personal use of an image.

Photos To Go
http://www.photostogo.com/

Over 200,000 images available for use, for a fee.

Getty Images
http://www.getty-images.com/

A starting-point for the resources of the Getty Images Corporation.

History and news images

Mirror Pix
http://www.mirrorpix.com/

Over 235,000 pictures from the Mirror Group newspapers' photo archive available online. There is a fee for using any of the images, but it is a useful resource for identifying images of people who have appeared in the news.

Time Inc Photo Collection
http://www.thepicturecollection.com/
An online searchable database of *Time Magazine*'s photo library. Registration to use the service is free and images can then be downloaded for use on a private computer only, but cannot be published in any format. The collection is very good for historical news photos.

Sporting images

Lots of fan pages contain many images for sports. The best approach to finding a relevant image is simply to find a fan page dedicated to that topic. The first example given below shows the type of material likely to be found on these pages. If a fan page doesn't provide the image you need, commercial sports picture libraries, like The Sports Archive, may be able to help.

Track Racing Photo Gallery
http://www.fatnick.com/picmain.htm

The Sport Archive
http://www.thesportarchive.com/

Animal and plant images

National History Museum Picture Library
http://www.nhm.ac.uk/piclib/

BBC Wild
http://www.bbcwild.com/
A commercial picture library with over 10,000 wildlife photographs available online.

Yahooligans – Downloader: Pictures: Animals and Nature
http://www.yahooligans.com/Downloader/Pictures/Animals___Nature/

Iowa State Entomology Image Gallery
http://www.ent.iastate.edu/imagegallery/

The Gardening Launch Pad Images
http://www.tpoint.net/neighbor/Pic.html
Collection of links to plant images.

Art images

Online galleries and museums

Artcyclopedia: The Guide to Museum Quality Art on the Internet
http://www.artcyclopedia.com/

Lists resources on the Internet on 5500 artists. Also lists an extensive number of galleries and museums on the Internet.

CGFA – Carol Gerten's Fine Art – A Virtual Art Museum
http://metalab.unc.edu/cjackson/index.html

A large collection of images of famous paintings organized by artist's name.

Fine Arts Museum of San Francisco Art Imagebase
http://www.thinker.org/fam/thinker.html

The Fine Arts Museum of San Francisco has a growing searchable online catalogue of its collections: paintings, drawings, etchings, porcelain, sculpture, silver, glass, furniture, textiles and more. The *Imagebase* now contains images of more than half of its collection. The aim is to have the whole collection online as soon as possible.

Louvre Museum Official Website
http://mistral.culture.fr/louvre/louvrea.htm

One of the better online gallery websites. A considerable number of paintings from its collection are available online (though of course only a tiny percentage of the gallery's complete collection). It is possible to download Quicktime movies to wander around the gallery virtually.

The Metropolitan Museum of Art
http://www.metmuseum.org/collections/

Selected images from New York's Metropolitan Museum of Art's collection. Resources have been catalogued and consequently detailed information, including provenance of articles, is provided.

Collage
http://collage.nhil.com/

An image database containing 20,000 works from the Guildhall Library and Guildhall Art Gallery, London.

National Gallery
http://www.nationalgallery.org.uk

National Portrait Gallery
http://www.npg.org.uk

Tate Galleries
http://www.tate.org.uk

Art image databases and archives

Mark Harden's Artchive
http://www.artchive.com/
Contains over 2000 fine art images. These images are available for personal non-profit, educational use.

Art.Com
http://www.art.com/
A commercial print and poster-selling company with a catalogue of 100,000 art prints available online. Very useful for finding art images quickly, in the same way that Amazon's catalogue can be used to confirm bibliographic details.

Architectural images

Cyburbia – Architecture Images and Exhibits
http://cyburbia.ap.buffalo.edu/
Cyburbia is a subject gateway for architecture resources and has a large collection of links to architecture images on the web.

National Monument Record Online Gallery
http://www.rchme.gov.uk/onlinegall.html
The National Monuments Record is the public archive of the Royal Commission on the Historical Monuments of England. It holds over 12 million items, including old and new photographs, maps, reports and surveys, and provides complete coverage of the country in aerial photographs. At present only a tiny proportion of this archive is available online, but there are plans to make more available as soon as possible. Part of its current work is the Images of England which is a photographic survey of every listed building in the UK. The aim is to have this 360,000 image collection on the Internet by 2002.

ArchInform – International Architecture Database
http://www.archINFORM.de/start.en.htm

This is the largest online database of architectural building projects and includes 8000 records. Some of these records contain images.

UW Digital Library Initiatives: Cities/Building Database
http://content.lib.washington.edu/cities/
Images of buildings in more than 30 countries. Access is geographically arranged. The aim is to create an electronic image archive on cities and architecture.

Scientific images

There are a number of very famous scientific image projects available on the web. The ability of the Internet to make data easily accessible anywhere around the world has meant that rare or previously difficult to find scientific images are easily available to all. This section only lists a few of the more famous projects, but often a simple search in a search engine will provide very useful resources.

The Visible Human Project
http://www.nlm.nih.gov/research/visible/
In 1989 the US National Library of Medicine began a project to create a databank of images of 1mm cross-sections of the whole of the human body.

Virtual Frog Dissection
http://www-itg.lbl.gov/vfrog/
A three-dimensional representation of the internal structure of a frog with animation and simulation.

NASA Image Exchange
http://nix.nasa.gov/
All kinds of space images here which are mainly not copyrighted.

Picture libraries and agencies

British Association of Picture Libraries and Agencies
http://www.bapla.org.uk/
BAPLA has an excellent directory of picture libraries in the UK – many of them listed with e-mail and web addresses – someone here is sure to have what you want.

16

Learning and education resources

- ★ General resources
- ★ News and current awareness
- ★ Learning resources
- ★ Careers information
- ★ Directories

New information and communications technologies are being exploited to enhance education and lifelong learning opportunities for all. With an increased emphasis on people taking responsibility for their own learning development and the continual learning and upgrading of skills throughout life, easy access to high quality information, advice and guidance is regarded as essential if people are to make the right learning and career choices. Electronic resources available over a widely accessible Internet will be central to realizing these aims.

The resources listed here are those concerned with engaging in the learning and education process as well as sites relating to more specific subject-related information.

General resources

DfEE website

http://www.dfee.gov.uk/

The site primarily provides documents produced by the Department. Access is via an A–Z site index. Information for teachers and governors is collected together in a dedicated area. A short list of links from here takes you to other primarily governmental education-related sites, such as the Department of Education for Northern Ireland and the Teacher Training Agency. The

Department covers education for England; Northern Ireland, Scotland and Wales have their own departments and websites at:

Department of Education Northern Ireland
http://www.deni.gov.uk/

Scottish Executive
http://www.scotland.gov.uk/

The National Assembly for Wales
http://www.wales.gov.uk/

Ofsted
http://www.ofsted.gov.uk/
Includes a database of all Ofsted reports of schools, which are normally available 12 weeks after inspection.

UCAS
http://www.ucas.ac.uk/
This is the UK universities and colleges admission service for the UK. The site currently provides entry requirements for institutions. A service is being developed that will allow applicants to view the progress of their application. Other services available on the site include information for prospective students about courses and institutions and data from UCAS for higher education staff.

The National Curriculum
http://www.dfee.gov.uk/nc/
Online document listing all curriculum requirements for five-to 16-year-olds in England. (Information on requirements for Wales, Scotland and Northern Ireland are available from the respective government offices/websites.)

NISS
http://www.niss.ac.uk/
NISS (National Information Services and Systems) provides online information services for the education and research community in the UK. Although NISS's primary target audience is higher education, users in further education and schools will also find valuable information via the *NISS* website. *NISS* provides many resources including online prospectuses, as well as offering links to other educational sites.

StudentUK
http://www.studentuk.co.uk/
A collection of articles and interactive services relevant to students. Draws on,

for example, the *Guardian* online service for the latest news, the *Independent* and the *Independent on Sunday* for current graduate jobs and the *Lonely Planet* for travel reports. UniverCity encourages communication through a chat room and a collection of personal profile pages of members (it's free to join). Gradubase is a searchable database of graduate employers.

News and current awareness

The Times Educational Supplement
http://www.tes.co.uk/
Online version of the print publication which includes substantial text from each week's edition. The TES Staffroom is a discussion area where you can post messages on a range of subjects. There is a searchable database of all vacancies as published in the printed version. A free Email Alert service will notify you of vacancies matching your job requirements profile. The TES Network has a Noticeboard advertising forthcoming conferences, events, exhibitions and courses. Also includes links to primary and secondary school websites. You can search editions of the *TES* back to 1994 in the TES Archive.

The Times Higher Education Supplement
http://www.thesis.co.uk/
Online version of the print publication. Although the site does not provide free access to the full text of the print publication, there are a number of free online-only services, such as a moderated discussion forum and a statistics section which includes research assessments and teaching quality listings for higher education. The Book Exchange puts people looking for a particular book in touch with anyone who has a copy for sale and Student Resources includes information on student life and help in navigating university quality ratings statistics.

Guardian Education
http://www.education.guardian.co.uk/
Articles from the *Guardian*'s weekly education supplement are enhanced with sections for parents, schools, colleges, HE and TEFL. Also includes features about using the Internet in the classroom, listings of recommended resources and children's book reviews.

Learning resources

The examples listed here are an attempt to show the variety and quality of resources that are available rather than to address all (or even limited) subject areas. More subject-specific sites can be found in other chapters of this part.

National Grid for Learning
http://www.ngfl.gov.uk/
The National Grid for Learning (NGfL) is a government initiative to support education, particularly lifelong learning. This site provides a gateway to information about education, such as local government sites which offer information on community education, as well as a database of learning resources. All sites in the Learning Resource Index have been assessed by the NGfL and brief descriptions of all indexed sites are provided.

BBC Education
http://www.bbc.co.uk/education/
The starting-point to the vast array of BBC education-related resources that are available. Sample resources include Home Learning, on the *Schools Online* website, which provides support and information for children and their parents learning at home. Many of the online resources draw from broadcast BBC educational material.

Ask a Librarian
http://www.earl.org.uk/ask/
An electronic reference service run by EARL, the consortium for public library networking. Questions sent to *Ask a Librarian* are distributed to participating EARL member libraries for responses. Previously asked questions and answers are available for reference.

GCSE Bitesize
http://www.bbc.co.uk/education/revision/
Includes notes, quizzes, chat forums and advice on revision for GCSEs. The website is one part of this BBC initiative that also includes related TV programmes.

BBC Knowledge
http://www.bbc.co.uk/knowledge/
BBC integrated online and TV channel devoted to 'tickling the fancy of the curious'. Interactive features include quizzes, discussion forums and an online novel to which users can contribute chapters.

www.a-levels.co.uk
http://www.a-levels.co.uk/
Collects together resources on popular A-level subjects from a variety of different sources.

Careers information

Advice on choosing a career and job-hunting can be combined with discovering information about potential employers. As well as company websites, the sites for trade and professional organizations, such as the TUC and the Institute of Information Scientists, can be useful sources of information.

Virtual Careers Library
http://www.kcl.ac.uk/kis/college/careers/links/links.htm
A collection of links to career-related sites provided by King's College London, including more than 1000 employer websites, self-employment, vacation work, work experience and voluntary work, regional and international working, and equal opportunities resources.

KCL Careers Service Helpsheets
http://www.kcl.ac.uk/kis/college/careers/helpshts.htm
Advice on various aspects of the job-seeking process, such as choosing a career, finding information and interview techniques. Links from here to other online services provided by the University of London.

Prospects Web
http://www.prospects.csu.ac.uk/
A guide to graduate careers and postgraduate study in the UK from the Higher Education Careers Services Unit. Provides advice on choosing careers, employers and research opportunities. *Prospects Direct* will deliver to you by e-mail job and research opportunities that match your requirements. And you can post your CV here for searching by potential employers.

Virtual Job Interview
http://www.careers.lon.ac.uk/advice/vintvw.htm
This service is provided by the University of London Careers Service and suggests answers to a number of standard interview questions.

Careers Information and Guidance on the Web
www.aiuto.net/uk.htm

A gateway for access to British web resources on careers information and guidance.

Examples of professional organizations

Institute of Chartered Accountants of England and Wales
http://www.icaew.co.uk/

Institute of Electrical Engineers
http://www.iee.org.uk/

Institute of Information Scientists
http://www.iis.org.uk/

Royal College of Nursing
http://www.rcn.org.uk/

Directories

UK Universities and Higher Education Colleges
http://www.ja.net/janet-sites/university.html
A listing of all UK higher education establishments, provided by JANET, the UK's academic and research network.

Further Education Colleges
http://bubl.ac.uk/uk/fe/
An index to over 540 further education colleges in the UK, arranged by name, region, county and type.

Universities Worldwide
http://geowww.uibk.ac.at/univ/
A searchable database provided by the University of Innsbruck of the home pages of almost 5000 universities in 142 countries.

Schoolsnet: Schools Guide
http://www.schoolsnet.com/
The Schools Guide provides basic facts and figures, including summary public examination results for over 5000 UK schools. *SchoolsNet* aims to be a 'virtual school rooted on the World Wide Web, at the heart of the National Grid for Learning'. A site to watch perhaps?

UK Public Libraries Page

http://dspace.dial.pipex.com/town/square/ac940/weblibs.html

As well as providing links to all public library websites, the site also provides pointers to other library-related resources that may be of interest, such as the *UK Web Library* (a searchable, classified catalogue of www pages at sites in the UK) and the Open University's International Centre for Distance Learning.

The British Library Catalogue

http://www.bl.uk/

The online link takes you to the British Library OPAC, where you can freely search the British Library's collection. Non-reference materials can be ordered by e-mail from the Document Supply Centre.

COPAC

http://copac.ac.uk/

COPAC provides access to the online catalogues of some of the largest university research libraries in the UK and Ireland. Records give details of holding libraries.

UK Lifelong Learning

http://www.lifelonglearning.co.uk/

The official government site to support lifelong learning. It brings together government reports, related advice and links on lifelong learning. There is an e-mail question and answer service and you can request regular e-mail updates on the website.

24 Hour Museum

http://www.24hourmuseum.org.uk/

A gateway to UK museums, galleries and heritage. Brief details such as address, opening times and descriptions of the collections are available from a database of over 2000 museum, gallery and heritage collections in the UK. The resources section will contain educational packs for parents, children and teachers. The Trails show attractions grouped by theme and geographical area. You can organize the content that you find through the *24 Hour Museum* by downloading the Scrapbook software. This helps you to navigate websites grouped by subject, organize bookmarks and read and make notes about websites. The *Y24* section is designed for younger children.

17

Literature resources

- ★ Online bookshops
- ★ Publishers
- ★ Popular authors
- ★ Academic resources
- ★ Creative writing
- ★ Electronic text collections
- ★ General literature/reading sites
- ★ Booktrade resources
- ★ Online reading groups

The Internet has much to offer the reader. Ranging from academic resources to online bookgroups, from virtual bookshops to fan pages, the scope and range of literature material are both fascinating and bewildering. This section on literature resources gives some idea of the type of material available.

Online bookshops

Online bookshops have exploited the interactivity of the web to allow visitors to their sites to talk about, write about and discuss the books they sell. Their huge million-of-items catalogues are a great place for quickly searching for bibliographical details of almost any book in print. As well as the giants like Amazon and Barnes and Noble, very small and specialized bookshops also have websites which provide information about their catalogues and bookstock.

Amazon.co.uk
http://www.amazon.co.uk/

Amazon.com
http://www.amazon.com/
The American branch which includes a recommendation centre.

Barnes and Noble
http://www.barnesandnoble.com/

The Internet Bookshop
http://www.bookshop.co.uk/

Yahoo's directory of online bookshops
http://uk.dir.yahoo.com/Business_and_Economy/Companies/Books/Shopping_and_Services/Booksellers/
(Information about searching out-of-print books is in Chapter 18).

Publishers

Publishers are beginning to use the Internet to provide information about their authors, books and promotions. Some of these sites are still very basic, whereas others provide resources for bookgroups, readers and librarians alike. A few of the better sites are included below.

HarperCollins
http://www.fireandwater.com/

Penguin
http://www.penguin.co.uk/

Random House
http://www.randomhouse.com/

Publishers' Catalogues Homepages
http://www.lights.com/publisher/
This is a web directory of publishers' websites around the world. It is comprehensive but not intuitive to use. Useful once you've got past the acres of advertising.

Popular authors

Many authors have web pages which provide information about them and heir works. These pages may be maintained by their publisher and be very lossy but impersonal. Others might be maintained by the author themselves nd be more personalized though less professional looking. A considerable umber of author pages have also been created by fans and again these range n quality and usefulness.

John Grisham Homepage
http://www.randomhouse.com/features/grisham/
Random House-produced site which contains information about John Grisham's latest book and information about the author – a fairly standard xample of the publisher-produced website.

Douglas Adams Village
http://www.douglasadams.com/
website overseen by Douglas Adams and an example of a more developed uthor-run site. The site provides information about Douglas Adams, news ems and the opportunity for fans to chat to each other via an online forum which Adams himself occasionally contributes to.

Anne Rice Homepage
http://www.annerice.com/
similar sort of site to the Douglas Adams one, but with the opportunity to download screensavers and join a mailing list. Not just a page about Anne Rice, but also a meeting place for her fans.

BookWire Author Indexes
http://www.bookwire.com/index/author-indexes.html
Jseful collection of links to a wide range of author-related web resources.

Authors at Yahoo!
http://uk.dir.yahoo.com/arts/Humanities/Literature/Authors/
Yahoo!'s section about literature also has a massive collection of links to pages bout authors – the quality of these resources will vary greatly, but again it's a great starting-point.

Academic resources

One excellent primary resource is the *Voice of the Shuttle* which has extensive coverage of literature resources on the web. It's been developed by Alan Liu, of the English Department at the University of California in Santa Barbara. Its focus tends to be more academic based than most of the resources previously discussed. Collections of resources range from Anglo-Saxon material to modern contemporary authors. Topics like semantics, literary theory and cultural studies are also covered.

Voice of the Shuttle
http://vos.ucsb.edu/

The English Server
http://eserver.org/
The English Server's primary function is to publish texts in the arts and humanities. The collections include art, architecture, drama, fiction, poetry, history, political theory, cultural studies, philosophy, women's studies and music.

Creative writing

The Internet is an ideal medium for the creative writer. Anyone can easily publish material online and make it available to a potentially global audience. The lack of face-to-face contact may also appeal to those would-be writers who are less willing to discuss or read their work with other people. The ease of communication on the Internet also allows people to share and discuss their work with each other, take part in virtual creative writing groups and even to take virtual creative writing courses.

Trace
http://trace.ntu.ac.uk/
A community in real and virtual space for writers and readers around the world – a UK site which is extremely nicely done.

Mailing Lists for Writers at Inkspot
http://www.inkspot.com/tk/network/mailing.html
A collection of mailing lists which discuss creative writing.

The Internet Writing Journal
http://www.writerswrite.com/journal/

Diarist.Net
http://www.diarist.net/
Lots of real people's online diaries.

Yahoo – Creative Writing
http://uk.dir.yahoo.com/arts/Humanities/Literature/Creative_Writing/
s always, *Yahoo!* provides a good place to start looking for resources.

lectronic text collections

here is a growing collection of complete texts which have been made avail-
ɔle on the Internet. Typically these are works of literature which are no longer
copyright and can be published in their entirety without legal complications.

Project Gutenberg
http://promo.net/pg/
ıst loads of stuff here – probably the best-known online archive of electronic
xts.

Electronic Text Centre
http://etext.lib.virginia.edu/
'his holds over 45,000 texts in 12 different languages with more than 50,000
lated images.

The On-line Books Page
http://digital.library.upenn.edu/books/
directory for electronic texts and projects involved with digitizing such mate-
al.

Stephen King's Riding The Bullet
http://www.simonandschuster.com/king/
tephen King's latest book (at the time of writing) was only available online in
ıe form of an e-book. Would-be readers have to pay $2.50 before they access it.

ieneral literature/reading sites

'here are many general literature sites on the web which aim simply to be
ntertainment for the reading enthusiast. These sites might contain reviews,
ompetitions, news, articles, first chapters and discussion groups. They operate
ke online magazines about reading. Typically sites of this kind might be a
ommercial enterprise, though there are some which are maintained by enthu-
iasts. There are also many sites of this kind which deal just with one particular
enre of literature.

BookBrowse
http://www.bookbrowse.com/
Excerpts from bestsellers and news about authors and events – aimed mainly at a US audience.

Bookbrowser
http://www.bookbrowser.com/
BookBrowser is a site dedicated to reading. It provides fiction reading lists, book reviews, forthcoming titles, author information and much more. It is maintained by two US librarians and again is aimed mainly at a US audience.

Mystery Reader
http://www.themysteryreader.com/
Mystery Reader is a genre-focused site about mystery novels.

Romance Reader
http://www.theromancereader.com/
Romance Reader is a genre-focused site about romance novels.

The Bookcase
http://www.bbc.co.uk/education/bookcase/
A collection of BBC online resources about reading – links into the 'Bookworm' programme and the Radio 4 Bookclub.

Charlotte Austin Review
http://www.charlotteaustinreview.com/
Book reviews, author interviews and short fiction.

Booktrade resources

The Bookseller
http://www.thebookseller.com/

London Review of Books
http://www.lrb.co.uk/

Book Industry Communication
http://www.bic.org.uk/

nline reading groups

here are many online reading groups on the Internet. These groups tend to perate via e-mail and follow a programme of reading which is discussed via a ailing list. These groups are very successful and many have been established r a number of years. Membership tends to be dominated by Americans, but ften with a wide sprinkling of other nationalities. Many publishers also pro- ide resources for bookgroups on their websites.

The Bookgroup List
http://books.rpmdp.com/
fairly typical list which runs via a mailing list. It is well organized and fol- ows a planned reading programme. Archives of previous discussions are vailable.

Baltimore County Public Library Bookclub
http://www.bcplonline.org/centers/library/bookclub.html
irtual bookclubs are also being set up by public libraries in order to cater for hose readers who can't make it to the library building.

The Bookwire Index – Reading Groups
http://www.bookwire.com/index/reading-groups.html
good list of different bookgroups – something for everyone here.

Vintage Reading Group Guides
http://www.randomhouse.com/vintage/read/list.html

Random House Reading Group Guides
http://www.bdd.com/resources/rgg.html

ook selection tools

ome web resources not only provide information about literature but also hoose your next book for you.

Forager
http://www.branching-out.net/forager/
Make a book selection based on your mood.

18

Reference resources

The number of reference questions that any public library reference desk can answer can be extensively expanded with access to the Internet. Even the smallest public library can have access to US phone directories, information about patents and the full text of the *Encyclopaedia Britannica*.

General resources

The amount of reference material which is available can be somewhat overwhelming, but there are a number of key websites which have organized the main resources into structured collections of links for use by reference librarians and members of the public around the world.

EARLweb

http://www.earl.org.uk/earlweb/

1RLweb is a collection of useful reference resources collected together by ARL – designed with the UK public librarian in mind.

Internet Public Library – Ready Reference Collection

http://www.ipl.org/ref/RR/

rge collection of extremely useful online reference resources – designed with e US librarian in mind.

Library Spot

http://www.libraryspot.com/

brary Spot is a commercial website which has been designed for librarians – aims to 'bring the best library and reference sites together with insightful editrial in one convenient, user-friendly spot'.

ıcyclopaedias

ost of the major encyclopaedias are now available in a CD-ROM format and creasingly these are also being made available online. Typically the online cyclopaedia will provide access to a small percentage of its resources for free d charge a subscription fee for access to the whole resource. However some these limited subsets may still be a major addition to a small library which es not have access to a printed version of a recent encyclopaedia.

Encyclopaedia Britannica Online

http://www.britannica.com

ıe complete text of the *Encyclopaedia Britannica* is available online for free. a onderful site which no library should be without.

Freeserve Encylopaedia

http://www.freeserve.co.uk/reference/encyclopaedia/

ıe *Freeserve Encyclopaedia*, which is based upon the *Cambridge Encyclopaedia* tabase, has over 35,000 thousand up-to-date articles, thousands of pictures d hundreds of sounds and animations.

Encarta

http://encarta.msn.com/

limited free version of Microsoft's multimedia encyclopaedia.

Hutchinson Online Encyclopaedia
http://www.bt-ern.co.uk/helicon/

Registering provides free access to a subset of the material available – a subscription is required for access to the whole encyclopaedia.

Encyclopaedia Mythica
http://www.pantheon.org/mythica/

This is an encyclopaedia of mythology, folklore, legends, and more. It contains over 5100 definitions of gods and goddesses, supernatural beings and legendary creatures and monsters from all over the world.

Statistics

National Office for Statistics
http://www.ons.gov.uk/

Includes access to *Statbase*, the UK national online statistics database.

UK Government Statistical Service
http://www.statistics.gov.uk/

Includes the UK in figures.

UK Census Gateway
http://census.ac.uk/

Still being developed at the time of writing.

CIA World Fact Book
http://www.odci.gov/cia/publications/factbook/index.html

The Data Archive
http://www.data-archive.ac.uk/

The Data Archive is a specialist national resource containing the largest collection of accessible computer-readable data in the social sciences and humanities in the UK.

Directories

YELL.com Directory
http://www.yell.co.uk/

Scoot
http://www.scoot.co.uk/

Directory of UK businesses which can be searched by business type and location.

Telephone Directories on the Web
http://www.teldir.com/

BT Phonenet UK
http://www.bt.com/phonenetuk/
British Telecom's white pages freely available on the Internet – business numbers also included, though the search mechanism is not as well designed as it could be.

UK Public Libraries Website Directory
http://dspace.dial.pipex.com/town/square/ac940/weblibs.html

UK Postcodes
http://www.afd.co.uk/pcsearch.htm

People Search – Yahoo's e-mail directory
http://ukie.people.yahoo.com/

Maps

Multimap.com
http://uk.multimap.com/
Enter a UK postcode and it brings up a map of that area. Can also be searched using place name, London streets and grid references.

Maps Website Directory
http://www.lib.utexas.edu/Libs/PCL/Map_collection/map_sites/map_sites.html
Developed by the Perry-Castañeda Library at the University of Texas, Austin, this is a huge collection of links to map resources on the web. It includes links to historical maps, city maps and weather maps.

Maps.com
http://www.maps.com/
A supplier of digital mapping services to industry, and an operator of map-based Internet destination and e-commerce sites for consumers, business and education. See also **http://www.mapquest.com** for a similar service.

Further map references are discussed in Chapter 20.

Biographies

World Biographical Index – Internet Edition
http://www.saur-wbi.de/

Gallery of Achievement
http://www.achievement.org/galleryachieve.html
A limited number, but useful nonetheless, of biographies of famous people of the 20th century.

Biographical Dictionary
http://www.s9.com/biography/
Over 27,000 people are listed in this resource.

Lives – the Biography Resource
http://amillionlives.com/
Huge collection of links to biography resources on the web.

News and media

UK TV channels

BBC
http://www.bbc.co.uk/
A very content-rich website which contains lots of useful information – the pages from BBC Education are particularly impressive.

ITV
http://www.itv.co.uk/

Channel 4
http://www.channel4.com/

Channel 5
http://www.channel5.co.uk/

Sky
http://www.sky.com/

Teletext
http://www.teletext.co.uk/
This site delivers the teletext service over the web instead of the TV.

Media UK Internet Directory
http://www.mediauk.com/directory/
A useful directory of UK Internet media resources – includes magazines, radio and television.

News

BBC News
http://news.bbc.co.uk/
Extensive and continually updated news website. It has a searchable archive which is building up into an extremely useful resource. One of the best sites available on the web.

CNN
http://europe.cnn.com/
Global news available for free online at CNN – mainly US focus.

ITN
http://www.itn.co.uk/

Ananova
http://www.ananova.com/
Created by the Press Association, Ananova is an online news site which has the world's first 'virtual newsreader'.

Reuters
http://www.reuters.com/news/

NewsNow
http://www.newsnow.co.uk/
Provides one access point to all the news stories from most of the major online news providers. A fast and convenient way to find out what's going on.

UK national newspapers

Most of the national newspapers now have websites. These sites may be an extension of their printed version which is continually updated during the day or may be only a limited copy of the print version. Most of the papers are free to access, but require you to register before you can use them.

Belfast Telegraph
http://www.belfasttelegraph.co.uk/

The Daily Mail
http://www.dailymail.co.uk/

Only the IT section is available online at the time of writing.

The Express
http://express.lineone.net/

Financial Times
http://www.ft.com/

The Guardian
http://www.guardian.co.uk/

The Independent
http://www.independent.co.uk/

The Mirror
http://www.mirror.co.uk/

The Observer
http://www.observer.co.uk/

The Scotsman
http://www.scotsman.com/

Sporting Life
http://www.sporting-life.com/

The Sun
http://www.the-sun.co.uk/

The Telegraph
http://www.telegraph.co.uk/

The Times
http://www.the-times.co.uk/

UK local papers

News Directory: UK
http://www.ecola.com/news/press/eu/uk/

A directory of UK newspapers including many local papers – an excellent esource for finding out what's happening locally all around the UK. Local ewspaper sites often provide access to job listings, property sales and local ntertainment and education information.

nternational newspapers

he Internet allows easy access to newspapers around the world for very little ost. Most newspapers are free to use although some like the *New York Times* equire you to register before you can use them. Like UK newspaper sites, ome are simply online versions of the print paper whilst others provide additi onal services and are continually updated through out the day. The *American ournalism Review (AJR)* is an extremely useful web directory of newspapers round the world.

AJR Newslink
http://ajr.newslink.org/news.html

All Newspapers.com
http://www.allnewspapers.com/
 commercial web directory of newspapers around the world that also includes inks to news agencies, magazines and television and radio stations.

Vhat's on

Film Finder
http://www.yell.co.uk/yell/ff/
 database of what films are showing where in the UK.

BBC Programme Alert
http://www.bbc.co.uk/alert/
The BBC's searchable directory of what's coming up on TV and radio. If you egister you can receive free weekly e-mails about programmes that are on vhich will be of interest to you.

Event Selector
http://www.eventselector.co.uk/
Event Selector is a free-to-use database of events around the UK. Material for the database is supplied by Press Association Listings.

Quotes

The Internet Movie Database Quote Search
http://us.imdb.com/Sections/quotes/
A database of famous quotation from recent films.

Bartlett Familiar Quotations (1901 Edition)
http://www.columbia.edu/acis/bartleby/bartlett/
The classic reference text freely available online, but limited by the fact that i uses the 1901 edition.

Quoteland
http://www.quoteland.com/
General site about quotes.

Dictionaries

There are a vast number of dictionaries available online, ranging from standard dictionaries to those specializing in specific topics such as medicine business and computing. A very useful search tool is the *One Look Dictionarie* which searches across 560 online dictionaries in one go. Medical dictionarie are listed in Chapter 13.

One Look Dictionaries
http://www.onelook.com/

WWWebster Dictionary
http://www.m-w.com/dictionary.htm
The *WWWebster Dictionary* is based on Merriam-Webster's *Collegiate*® *Dictionary*, tenth edition and is freely available.

Brewer's Dictionary of Phrase and Fable (1894 edition)
http://www.bibliomania.com/Reference/PhraseAndFable/

Symbol Dictionary
http://www.symbols.com/
Contains more than 2500 different symbols which can be searched for o browsed.

The Rap Dictionary
http://www.rapdict.org/
Rap song terminology explained!

Nolo.com Law Dictionary
http://www.nolo.com/dictionary/wordindex.cfm
Legal terms explained in simple language – covers American law.

RhymeZone: The Semantic Rhyming Dictionary
http://www.rhymezone.com/

Roget's Thesaurus (1852 Edition)
http://www.thesaurus.com/

Entertainment

There are a considerable number of useful online databases about film and music. These databases are free to use though they are commercial sites and might be trying to sell you videos and CDs at the same time.

Internet Movie Database
http://uk.imdb.com/
The biggest and the best of the movie reference tools.

All Music
http://www.allmusic.com/
Information can be searched for by song name, album name, artist, style and label. It has a sister site called *All Classical* (**http://allclassical.com**), containing only data on classical music which can be searched by performer or composer.

Ultimate Bandlist
http://www.ubl.com/
Huge web directory of pop music resources. Simply searching on the name of a group will provide a collection of web resources dedicated solely to that group.

Nom de Guerre – The Real People's Real Name Resource of Pseudonyms and Aliases
http://www.walshnet.com/walshnet/punster/realname.htm

International Lyrics Server
http://www.lyrics.ch/
Database of lyrics mainly from pop music.

Other material

Patent Office
http://www.patent.gov.uk/

Acronym Finder
http://www.acronymfinder.com/
Over 100,000 acronyms explained here – including UKOLN!

Homesight
http://www.homesight.co.uk/
By entering a postcode you can find out about the schools, amenities and council tax of any area of the country.

Out-of-print books

A very useful resource is the increasing number of websites created by independent bookshops specializing in out-of-print and rare books. These sites consist of a union catalogue of the holdings of a large number of bookshops. This enables out-of-print and rare books to be tracked down quickly. Books can easily be purchased with a credit card and they are delivered through the post. An easy way to track down a nostalgic birthday gift of a 1960s pop-up Babar book or a hard-to-find reader request. Most of these sites and the bookshops that contribute to them are in the USA. This raises the delivery charges of each item to UK users but doesn't decrease the speed of the service.

Abebooks.com – the World's Network of Independent Booksellers
http://www.abebooks.com/

Bibliofind
http://www.bibliofind.com/

Booksearch Biglink
http://www.booksearch.com/

Bookfinder
http://www.bookfinder.com/

Yahoo's listing of UK Out of Print Booksellers
http://uk.dir.yahoo.com/Regional/Countries/United_Kingdom/Business_and_Economy/Shopping-and-Services/Books/Booksellers/Antique-Rare-and-Used/

Reference help

There are a number of online newsgroups or services provided by librarians to help either other librarians or members of the public to answer those impossible reference queries. These services depend on the cooperation of reference librarians who field queries by e-mail.

Ask A Librarian
http://www.earl.org.uk/ask/index.html
Ask A Librarian is managed by EARL, the UK public library consortium. A number of reference libraries around the UK take it in turns to answer reference queries which are submitted through the main page of the site.

Stumpers Mailing List
http://www.cuis.edu/~stumpers/
A mailing list for reference librarians around the world who help each other out with those hard-to-answer reference questions.

Ask An Expert
http://www.askanexpert.com/
A collection of links to experts in a large number of fields who are willing to answer questions online.

Deja.com
http://www.deja.com/usenet/
Deja.com hosts and provides access to over 40,000 discussion forums. The archives of these forums are searchable through the main *Deja.com* site and consequently provide access to a vast repository of what can be very specialized knowledge.

19

Science and technology resources

- ★ General resources
- ★ Engineering
- ★ Chemistry
- ★ Biology
- ★ Physics
- ★ Environment
- ★ Science news
- ★ Magazines
- ★ Space/astronomy
- ★ Inventors/inventions/patents
- ★ Scientists

Internet science and technology resources are very numerous and for this section just a number of 'taster sites' have been chosen. One of the benefits of the Internet is that it makes information about very specialized topics accessible to a vast number of people. Every branch of science and technology, every topic and every research area is probably covered in some form on the Internet. As well as web pages of information, actual scientists and researchers themselves are also accessible via e-mail (though they may not necessary reply!). The Internet allows people both to read about science and also to discuss it and swap ideas.

General resources

General science sites are often the best starting-point for finding information on a particular topic. Most of the sites listed below provide useful collections of categorized science links.

New Scientist Key Websites
http://www.keysites.com/keysites/hotspots/hotspots.html
An excellent list of useful science sites on the Internet.

Tomorrow's World
http://www.bbc.co.uk/tw/
All the latest news from the 'Tomorrow's World' team.

ScienceNet
http://www.sciencenet.org.uk/
ScienceNet is a free science information service, staffed by scientists who are expert in explaining complex topics in everyday language.

SciSeek
http://www.sciseek.com/
A very useful directory for online science resources.

SciCentral
http://www.scicentral.com/
A gateway to science and engineering resources available online.

The Science Explorer
http://library.advanced.org/11771/english/hi/
Learning units on different scientific topics.

How Stuff Works
http://www.howstuffworks.com/
Find out exactly how your toilet works and get to ask questions too – a really good resource.

NISS Lecture Theatre
http://www.niss.ac.uk/lt/
Collections of science links for a UK audience from NISS.

Engineering

Electronic Engineering Virtual Library (EEVL)
http://www.eevl.ac.uk/
Subject gateway for engineering resources on the Internet.

Engineering at Yahoo!
http://uk.dir.yahoo.com/science/engineering/
A useful starting-point which has categorized links into lots of different areas of engineering.

Engineering Electronic Library
http://eels.lub.lu.se/
An information system for quality-assessed Internet resources in the technical sciences.

Chemistry

Chemdex
http://www.chemdex.org
The major gateway to chemistry resources on the web.

ChemNet
http://listen.to/chemistry/
ChemNet provides access to datafiles and information about all branches of chemistry, famous chemists and the history of chemistry. Contains a useful guide to other chemistry resources on the web.

Tables of Chemical Data
http://www.chem.ualberta.ca/courses/plambeck/p101/p0040x.htm

Biology and botany

Anatomically Correct Cat Dissection
http://library.advanced.org/15401/

BioMedNet
http://www.biomednet.com/
The Internet community for biological and medical researchers – a free service which requires you to register.

CTI Centre for Biology
http://www.liv.ac.uk/ctibiol.html
Contains useful links to online biology learning resources.

Institute of Biology
http://www.iob.org/
The primary UK biology organization.

Internet Directory for Botany
http://www.botany.net/IDB/
A huge collection of botany links, arranged alphabetically rather than by topic.

Biolinks
http://www.biolinks.com/
Biological links collection.

Physics

Physical Reference Data
http://physics.nist.gov/PhysRefData/
Data for physicists.

PhysLINK.com
http://www.physlink.com/
Aims to provide comprehensive research and education tools for physicists, engineers, educators, students and all other curious minds.

World-Wide Web Virtual Library – Physics
http://www.vlib.org/Physics.html
Lots of physics links.

American Journal of Physics
http://ojps.aip.org/
The leading physics journal.

Reviews of Modern Physics
http://rmp.aps.org/
The online version of the well-known physics journal.

High Energy Physics Information Centre
http://www.hep.net/
Designed to help high energy physics researchers around the world.

Institute of Physics
http://www.iop.org/
The website of the Institute of Physics provides online access to many of its physics journals.

PhysicsWeb
http://physicsweb.org/
Global news and information about physics.

TIPTOP
http://physicsweb.org/TIPTOP/
The Internet Pilot to Physics – useful collection of physics links on the web.

Environment

Natural Environment Research Council
http://www.nerc.ac.uk/

Greenpeace
http://www.greenpeace.org.uk/

Friends of the Earth
http://www.foe.co.uk/
Includes Factory Watch which gives you information about your local polluting factories.

GreenNet
http://www.gn.apc.org/
Networking for the environment, peace, human rights and development.

EnviroLink
http://www.envirolink.org/
EnviroLink is dedicated to providing the most comprehensive, up-to-date environmental resources available.

Science news

PopSci
http://www.popsci.com/
Popular science – information for anyone with a vague interest in science.

BBC News: Sci/Tech
http://news.bbc.co.uk/hi/english/sci/tech/
The latest science news from BBC News.

CNN Technology
http://cnn.com/TECH/
The latest science news from CNN.

Discovery Online News
http://www.discovery.com/news/news.html
The latest science news from the Discovery Channel.

SPIN
http://wisdom.wellcome.ac.uk/wisdom/spinhome.html
Searchable database on science policy news items from 1992 to present.

Magazines

Many science magazines also have online versions.

National Geographic
http://www.nationalgeographic.com/

Nature
http://www.nature.com/

New Scientist
http://www.newscientist.com/

Space/astronomy

There appear to be huge amounts of space and astronomy information available on the Internet. NASA in particular has developed extensive websites which provide the latest information about all of their different projects, some which contain absolutely stunning freely available content.

NASA
http://www.nasa.gov/

A Space Library
http://samadhi.jpl.nasa.gov/
Images and programs from NASA which help you visualize the solar system.

Heavens Above
http://www.heavens-above.com/
Tells you when you'll be able to see satellites passing overhead.

Online Astronomer
http://astronomer.net/
This site is intended for the amateur astronomer who is just getting started and is looking for some basic information.

Spacezone
http://www.spacezone.com/
Information on all things space.

Florida Today Space Online
http://www.flatoday.com/space/
Up-to-the-minute news of space happenings in Florida.

Inventors/inventions/patents

Patent information is often freely and easily available online – a true revolution, meaning that even the smallest library can provide their users with access to the latest patent information from around the world.

UK Patent Office
http://www.patent.gov.uk/
The Patent Office provides free access to the published patent application databases of the UK Patent Office, the European Patent Office and other European national patent offices, as well as access to the PCT database of published patent applications.

US Patent and Trademark Office – Database
http://www.uspto.gov/patft/

European Patent Office
http://www.european-patent-office.org/

IBM Intellectual Property Network
http://patent.womplex.ibm.com/ibm.html
The Intellectual Property Network (IPN) lets you search and view patent documents from the USA, Europe and Japan as well as patent applications published by the World Intellectual Property Organization (WIPO).

The Great Idea Finder
http://www.ideafinder.com/
A general site about inventing and inventions.

The National Inventors Hall of Fame
http://www.invent.org/
National meaning American.

Institute of Inventors
http://members.aol.com/mikinvent/index.html
UK-based organization.

Women Inventors
http://www.inventorsmuseum.com/women.htm

National Endowment for Science and the Arts (NESTA)
http://www.nesta.org.uk/
JK government scheme to encourage innovation – application forms available online.

Scientists

Many famous scientists have websites and e-mail addresses – you may not get a personal response, but the Internet does provides an easy means to contact people such as Stephen Hawkings and Tim Berners Lee directly.

Yahoo! Science – People
http://uk.dir.yahoo.com/science/people
A good starting-point for tracking down the scientific person.

Four Hundred Years of Women in Science
http://www.astr.ua.edu/4000WS/

Stephen Hawking
http://www.hawking.org.uk/

Tim Berners Lee
http://www.w3.org/People/Berners-Lee/
Inventor of the world wide web.

20

Travel resources

- ★ Transport guides
- ★ Travel writing and destination guides
- ★ Accommodation guides
- ★ General information and advice
- ★ Maps
- ★ Foreign languages

There is much commercial activity on the Internet in travel-related areas. Established travel companies and an increasing number of exclusively web-based companies offer the opportunity to purchase all manner of travel-related products, such as tickets, accommodation and holidays online. Although this section will concentrate on travel-related information rather than commercial transactions, you will find that many sites primarily providing free information will also be offering the opportunity to purchase products from retailers in related areas.

Transport guides

These guides can be particularly useful compared with print-based equivalents, especially when making complicated journeys with many changes of route. In addition to timetables, some sites allow you to book tickets online. Most will provide regularly updated news of disruptions to services. In addition to these major, national services, a number of local public transport companies publish their timetables on the Internet.

UK Public Transport Information
http://www.pti.org.uk/

This index provides links to all the main UK transportation websites, including some of those listed separately below. Links to some bus companies operating local services can also be found.

Railtrack
http://www.railtrack.co.uk/travel/
The online timetable for all UK public train services. Very quick and easy to obtain timetable information, particularly when compared with searching the printed alternatives.

National Express
http://www.nationalexpress.co.uk/
Once you have planned your journey using the timetable and checked the fare, you can book tickets online.

Eurostar
http://www.eurostar.co.uk/
This site allows you to book tickets and access timetables and information on fares and special offers.

London Transport
http://www.londontransport.co.uk/
Information such as current repair work and disruptions to services for London's bus, underground and light railway services. Underground maps and details of bus routes are available and a journey planner is being developed.

Airwise: the Airport and Air Travel Guide
http://www.airwise.com/
Airline, airport and aviation industry news; includes a facility to allow you to check arrival times for major worldwide airlines and provides a forum for discussion of airline passenger rights.

RAC Online Services
http://www.rac.co.uk/services/
The route planner will find you a route between selected destinations throughout Europe and report on the traffic conditions along the route. Once you have selected your route you can have the latest traffic news along the route delivered to you by e-mail before you leave on your journey.

Travel writing and destination guides

Many of the guides listed here will be familiar as print-based publications and although the information contained in the website may not differ substantially from that in the print-based publication, the sites chosen as examples here demonstrate the extent to which interactivity can enhance the delivery of information.

International

Brits Abroad

http://www.geocities.com/TheTropics/2865/

Useful links to immigration services in the USA, Australia, New Zealand, Japan and South Africa, as well as selected British cultural and historical highlights.

The CIA World Factbook

http://www.odci.gov/cia/publications/factbook/

The US Central Intelligence Agency makes available to the public information on the geography, people, government, economy, communications, transportation and the military in many countries.

Fodor's Travel Online

http://www.fodors.com/

Website of the well-known print publication. Allows you to create personalized city guides to places to stay, eat and visit from the information held on the site. Travellers provide advice in the forum section.

Journeywoman

http://www.journeywoman.com/

A resource designed for women travellers. Destination reports and advice on travelling, eating and sleeping safely, especially for women travelling alone. Contributions are encouraged from readers and you can subscribe to a free e-mail newsletter. *HERmail.net* is designed to connect people with similar interests. You connect, privately, through the website, so personal e-mail addresses are not disclosed.

Lonely Planet Online

http://www.lonelyplanet.com/

As well as text from the print publication and regularly updated travel news, there are tales, tips and advice posted by travellers from their own experiences, ncluding the not-so-pleasant aspects encountered while travelling. There is a liscussion forum covering all aspects of travel.

National Geographic Traveler

http://www.nationalgeographic.com/traveler/

Web magazine of the National Geographic Society with feature articles and ips and advice from travellers via the e-mail discussion forum.

PlanET

http://www.the-planet.co.uk/

This is the travel section of the web version of the *Daily Telegraph* and contains he articles and reports published in the newspaper.

Rough Guide to Travel

http://travel.roughguides.com/

Text from the well-known print publication. Interactive features including a weekly e-mail newsletter and a bulletin board.

Salon Travel

http://www.salon.com/travel/

The site offers original features and news updates and will answer your travel-related questions. Readers can contribute their own writings to the site. There are links to sites where you can book accommodation and other travel services. *Salon.com* is an online magazine with travel being one of a number of topics covered. The Tabletalk area provides opportunities for online discussions and participation.

Time Asia

http://cnn.com/ASIANow/time/

News stories as well as travel information from Asia from the website of *Time* magazine. Includes material exclusive to the website.

Tourism Concern

http://www.tourismconcern.org.uk/

Information and articles about the work of the UK-based campaign for fair, sustainable and responsible tourism.

World Heritage

http://www.unesco.org/whc/

A complete listing of all UNESCO World Heritage sites. Virtual tours are available of a selection of sites.

UK

The British Tourist Authority
http://www.visitbritain.com/
The official site of the British Tourist Authority. Provides an overview of tourist-related information for Britain. Particularly good for overseas visitors and the site is available in a number of foreign languages.

Complete Guide to Irish Tourism
http://www.infosites.net/tourism/
Part of a larger site devoted to all things Irish from the *Irish Times*.

The Lake District
http://www.lake-district.gov.uk/
Information about the landscape and scenery of the lakes as well as tourist information listings.

UK Travel Guide
http://www15.pair.com/cir/
A gateway to travel and tourism information and services provided by UK towns and cities. London has its own separate guide. The site was originally developed by University College London.

Accommodation guides

Listed below is a selection of the many guides to finding accommodation that are available on the web. The amount of information provided about individual places will vary. E-mail booking facilities are available for a number of establishments.

AA Accommodation Guide
http://www.theaa.co.uk/hotels/
Includes a list of AA-inspected places to eat in the UK as well as the accommodation guide.

Accommodation Search Engine
http://ase.net/
A search engine that covers over 60,000 accommodation web pages worldwide.

Searchhotels.com
http://www.searchhotels.com/
A worldwide accommodation search engine.

Lastminute.com

http://www.lastminute.com

As its name suggests, last-minute deals on hotels, flights, gifts, holidays and ther entertainments.

General information and advice

There are many sites dedicated to providing health information and advice for ravellers. Many of the sites provide information from official government ources. The more informative sites will also provide information about genral health-related issues such as climate and social conditions.

Foreign and Commonwealth Travel Advice

http://www.fco.gov.uk/travel/

The latest UK official advice about countries to which it is unsafe to travel is vailable here. The site also includes a directory of consular services worldwide nd visa information for people coming into the UK.

Travel Health Online

http://www.tripprep.com/

A comprehensive listing of health-related information for a large number of ountries. Included is general information about the country's climate, location and geography, health precautions travellers should take when visiting and official health data for the country from the World Health Organization. This s a US site and some information, such as entry requirements, are for US citizens only. However, this is still a good source of general, country-specific health-related information. Much of the information is from official (US) government sources.

Medical Advisory Services for Travellers Abroad

http://www.masta.org/

MASTA was set up by the London School of Hygiene and Tropical Medicine to aise awareness of health issues associated with travel. Provides a wide range of health advice, including recommended immunizations, descriptions of symptoms and treatments for the more common ailments.

Traveler's Health

http://www.cdc.gov/travel/

Lots of country-specific health information from the US Centers for Disease Control and Prevention.

Help For World Travelers!
http://www.kropla.com/

All those things you never remember when travelling, until it's too late! The site includes worldwide guides to electricity supplies (so you know just what plug to take with you), international dialling codes and a guide to connecting modems to phone systems. Pictures of plugs and phone connections are particularly useful.

BBC Weather Centre
http://www.bbc.co.uk/weather/

The site provides five-day UK and international forecasts, the shipping forecasts and UK satellite images, monthly rainfall, temperature and sunshine reports, as well as weather-related features. Data is supplied by the UK Meteorological Office.

Local Times Around the World
http://times.clari.net.au/

A listing of local time in all of the world's countries and many of its islands. The site also provides geographical locations.

The Embassy Web
http://www.embpage.org/

A searchable database of diplomatic posts worldwide with links to websites of offices where available. At the time of writing the site is undergoing revision and promises to be a useful, comprehensive resource.

The Currency Site
http://www.oanda.com/

A comprehensive site that provides current exchange rates as well as historical rates and forecasts for future world currencies.

Maps

A vast range of maps to places all around (and beyond!) the world is accessible. The selection shown here include road maps, maps of administrative areas and astrological maps.

Ordnance Survey
http://www.ordsvy.gov.uk/

. particularly useful area of this site is Get-a-map. You are allowed free access) maps up to 1:250,000 scale covering the whole of Britain.

Oddens's Bookmarks: The Fascinating World of Maps and Mapping
http://oddens.geog.uu.nl/
'his site collects links to maps, atlases and related cartographic information for ll parts of the world and universe beyond!

Mapquest
http://www.mapquest.com/
'rovides maps to over three million locations worldwide. The site also provides riving directions, can overlay places of interest and you can create and save ersonalized maps.

The UK Street Map Page
http://www.streetmap.co.uk/
'rom this site you can access street maps for London and road atlas maps for he whole of mainland Britain. Searching is by postcode and street/place name.

Expedia Maps
http://maps.expedia.com/overview.asp/
\ good way to find maps and related travel and tourist information on places nywhere in the world. Some other services, such as locating addresses and riving directions, are for the USA only.

'oreign languages

There are a number of sites that can translate text and provide useful translaions. Although, with English being the prevalent language of the Internet, nost services provide translations to or from English.

Foreign Languages for Travelers
http://www.travlang.com/languages/
Translations of simple words and phases from over 70 languages. Sound files ielp with pronunciation.

AltaVista translation service
http://babelfish.altavista.digital.com/
Translates text, including whole web pages. Languages are limited: English can be translated to or from French, German, Italian, Spanish and Portuguese;

the translations aren't always grammatically correct, but this is an extremely useful tool nonetheless.

21

₹esources for professional use

- Library organizations on the web
- Current awareness
- Web directories of library resources
- Library and information science journals
- Funding
- Career development

.ibrary organizations on the web

Iany of the sites selected here will be well known to those working in the UK ublic library community, others will be less so, having, as they do, academic brary or non-UK origins. These have been included, however, as they often ave much to offer public libraries as, broadly speaking, Internet use is more videly developed in the academic sector and in the USA. Many of the issues hat public libraries are now grappling with as they begin to develop networked ervices, are similar to those that have already been identified and explored in ther sectors.

JK

Aslib
http://www.aslib.co.uk/
.llows online ordering of some of its publications. Access to a number of Aslib ournals is available if you are a subscriber. If not, access is limited to content ages and abstracts (although access to the electronic version of *Managing*

Information is unrestricted). Full information is provided about the range of training courses that are available and there is access to *Prospects*, the monthly recruitment paper. The What's New section provides a useful update of additions to the website.

The British Library Document Supply Centre
http://portico.bl.uk/dsc/
The website allows you to search the British Library catalogue and order documents and request loans online.

CERLIM
http://www.mmu.ac.uk/h-ss/cerlim/
The Centre for Research in Library and Information Management based a Manchester Metropolitan University. A number of the projects that the centre works on will have relevance in the public sector. Project information and reports can be accessed from the site.

CONARLS: Circle of Officers of National and Regional Library Systems
http://www.zebra.co.uk/conarls/
CONARLS supports the development of cooperation services between regional library services in the UK. The website provides access to a number of CONARLS reports and publications.

The Department for Culture, Media and Sport: Libraries
http://www.culture.gov.uk/heritage/
The website brings together the UK governmental responsibilities for public libraries, with links to key government documents and related organizations.

EARL
http://www.earl.org.uk/
EARL provides a range of services, and support for library networking activities. The Networked Services Policy Taskgroup, for example, have produced a series of issue papers in key areas of development and delivery of networked services in public libraries. Get Online is a directory of public libraries offering Internet access to the public in the UK. Other services have been developed dealing with community and European Union information, and non-English language library materials. Ask a Librarian is a national reference enquiry service for the public where e-mailed enquiries are answered by EARL member libraries. *EARLweb* is a collection of Internet resources covering areas such a lifelong learning, imagination and memory, and online reference.

eLib: The Electronic Libraries Programme

http://www.ukoln.ac.uk/services/elib/

'he eLib funding programme supports the development and implementation f the electronic library in the higher education community. Since its inception 1995 more than 60 projects have been funded to investigate issues surrounding moves towards the concept of the electronic library, access to network esources, electronic document delivery and training and awareness. The website provides links to all the projects funded by the programme as well as news f the programme itself. Although focused on the higher education sector, a umber of projects have produced much that could well be taken on board in he public sector, as public libraries encounter many of the same problems and ssues as HE in the transition towards the electronic library service.

Forum for Inter Lending

http://www.la-hq.org.uk/liaison/fil/introf.html

Contact details and information about events the Forum organizes.

Information North

http://www.ris.niaa.org.uk/heritage-north/info-north/

nformation North is a UK cooperative of regional library and information rganizations. The website provides information about the organization and he RIS project – described as 'The North's "New Library" Network'.

The Institute of Information Scientists

http://www.iis.org.uk/

Provides basic information about the Institute.

Interlending Wales

http://seren.newi.ac.uk/cciw/index1.htm

Useful resources on this site include access to Welsh library-related sites and public library catalogues in Wales. There are a number of discussion papers elated to interauthority cooperation.

LASER

http://www.viscount.org.uk/laser/

LASER is a networking agency for UK libraries and the website is used to advertise the consultancy, advice, research and development and training services that the organization offers. There is also information about the research projects that LASER is involved in.

The Library & Information Statistics Unit
http://www.lboro.ac.uk/departments/dils/lisu/lisuhp.html
LISU provides statistical information about public, academic and specia libraries in the UK. The website provides access to extracts from its reports an guides such as 'Who else writes like . . .?', along with their annual statistics which cover such things as staffing levels, opening hours, most borrowe authors, etc.

Resource
http://www.resource.gov.uk/
Resource, The Council for Museums, Archives and Libraries, is a strategi agency working with museums, archives and libraries in the UK.

The Library Association
http://www.la-hq.org.uk/
The website provides access to LA documents produced on library and infor mation issues, such as responses to Government initiatives, summaries o legislation and reports by the Association. Some information about LA publi cations is also available. The site hosts online discussion forums in areas o current interest and also one aimed at the solo LIS worker. Probably the mos useful parts of the website are the news and careers sections, which are dis cussed later in this chapter. Only the contents pages of the *LA Record* ar available online.

Library Link Home Page
http://www.mcb.co.uk/liblink/
Library Link is a commercial online information and discussion forum fo information management. It is UK based, but has an international perspective Although you have to subscribe to access some of the online journals there ar still a lot of information and discussion areas that are accessible to non-sub scribers. The Librarian's Digest, for example, allows free access to on library-related article from the latest edition of one of the journals published b MCB.

National Library of Scotland
http://www.nls.ac.uk/
Provides access to a number of online catalogues and a selection of th Library's items that have been digitized.

North West Regional Library System
http://www.nwrls.org.uk/
The site contains information about the organization's services and projects.

SLAINTE: Scottish Libraries across the Internet
http://www.slainte.org.uk/
This is the website of the Scottish Library Association and the Scottish Library and Information Council and provides information on people, organizations, libraries, events, and resources of Scottish interest. Included is biographical information on 80 Scottish authors. There is also a searchable database of community information.

The Society of Chief Librarians of England and Wales
http://www.chieflib.org/
The site provides information about the constitution of the organization and its activities.

UK Office for Library and Information Networking (UKOLN)
http://www.ukoln.ac.uk/
The Public Library Networking area provides links to projects and initiatives that the UK Office for Library and Information Networking are involved in, including *Stories from the Web*, a children's library Internet service model. Among the UKOLN-produced resources is a downloadable training pack for library staff about the influential report *New Library: The People's Network* (UKOLN hosts the online version of *New Library* on behalf of the LIC) and materials for running an Internet introductory session for the public. Links are provided to presentations given and publications produced by the public library research staff. Other areas of the UKOLN website are concerned with the broader issues of network information management, such as resource discovery, web technologies and interoperability across information sectors, including libraries and the cultural heritage and archival communities.

West Midlands Regional Library System
http://www.wm-libraries.org.uk/wmrls.htm
Links to development projects, such as *Lit-Net*, a virtual literature centre offering services for readers, writers, librarians and literature professionals.

Non-UK

The American Library Association
http://www.ala.org/

Information about the work that the Association does and the way it is organized. LIS publications can be bought from the online store, which also sells promotional products such as T-shirts and stationery. A number of online fact sheets are available including 'Marketing to Libraries' and 'How many libraries are on the Internet?'.

Berkley Digital Library SunSite
http://sunsite.berkeley.edu:80/

This US-based website provides information and support for digital library developers. Links to digital library projects, training materials and information about software tools. The Information section provides a useful list of links to digital library information resources such as standards for digital library development, preservation, metadata and copyright and intellectual property.

European Union digital heritage and cultural content programme
http://www.cordis.lu/ist/ka3/digicult/

This is one of the main library, museum and archive-related areas of research of the EC's Information Society Technologies (IST) programme. As well as the latest news about, for example, funding calls, the website provides background to the research programme and support activities.

The International Federation of Library Associations and Institutions
http://ifla.inist.fr/

Provides information and reports on current and past projects and initiatives. There is a whole section devoted to public libraries. The collection of electronic resources includes resources on digital libraries, information policy, the Internet and networking, as well as some more light-hearted library humour and quotations.

Libraries for the Future
http://www.lff.org/

This is a US organization dedicated to information equity, literacy and the preservation and renewal of libraries as essential tools for a democratic society. The website offers a glimpse at the advocacy work and research projects that the organization supports. The information itself is of most relevance to US libraries.

urrent awareness

ıe immediacy of the Internet means that is it an excellent way to keep up to te with latest news and developments. Selected here are a mixture of news es, many from well-known library organizations, and mailing lists. Subribing to a mailing list provides you with the opportunity of sharing ıowledge, expertise and discussion with people of similar interests regardless geographic location. These can be moderated, where the list owner checks l messages (usually for appropriateness), although many selected here are ımoderated. Lists will usually have guidelines and posting policies that ould be followed so that discussion remains 'on topic'. Users of lists are usuly encouraged to share the information that they may collect from other list embers. Some lists operate digests whereby you receive all messages posted to e list at regular intervals, such as once a day, as one long message with a table contents at the top. In the UK, Mailbase hosts over 2000 discussion lists, priarily aimed at the higher education community, but some will be relevant to ose in the public library sector.

UK-based public library-related Mailbase lists
lis-publib-research@mailbase.ac.uk
n unmoderated list focusing on current and recent research in public oraries.

lis-pub-libs@mailbase.ac.uk
forum for discussion of topics of general interest (with a particular focus on etworked services) to public librarians in the UK and elsewhere. UK-based nmoderated list.

lis-ill@mailbase.ac.uk
list for anyone interested in interlibrary loans or document delivery.

Web4Lib
web4lib@sunsite.berkeley.edu
list for library-based web managers. The list is for the discussion of issues ıch as website design, cataloguing and metadata issues regarding web inforıation, creating and maintaining secure public web stations and training staff r users to use the web. It is an unmoderated list, but only subscribers may post ıessages. US-based.

PUBLIB

publib@sunsite.berkeley.edu

A list for public librarians and those interested in public libraries.

PUBLIB-NET

publib-net@sunsite.berkeley.edu

PUBLIB-NET, a subset of *PUBLIB*, including only those posts related to th Internet in public libraries. Both *PUBLIB* and *PUBLIB-NET* are US-base moderated lists, and messages can be received once a day in a digest.

Newsgroups can also be a good way of keeping in touch and sharing idea A good source of library-related groups can be found in the *BUBL News* se vice:

http://www.bubl.ac.uk/news/lisgroups.htm

Library Association News

http://www.la-hq.org.uk/hot_news/

These Hot News pages provide the latest news stories from the LIS commu nity. Other current awareness services on the site include new titles from L Publishing, a 'what's on' calendar section and online discussion groups.

EARL News

http://www.earl.org.uk/news/

Relevant items of latest news are published and an online newsletter provide updates on new library developments. EARL press releases and responses t Government initiatives are also available.

Department for Culture, Media and Sport press releases

http://www.nds.coi.gov.uk/

This is the press release section of the Central Office of Information's websit which lists all government organizations. From here you can go to th Department for Culture, Media and Sport's listing.

BUBL News

http://www.bubl.ac.uk/news/

The *BUBL News* service rounds up items that have previously been posted t various library-related Mailbase mailing lists. Areas covered are jobs, event survey reports, offers and requests, and recent additions to the BUBL servic In addition, this site links to library-related Usenet newsgroups.

Resource News
http://www.resource.gov.uk/news/
News from Resource, the Council for Museums, Archives and Libraries.

Library Link News
http://www.liblink.co.uk/news.html
The News section of *Library Link* (see 'Library Organizations on the web' section above for a fuller description of this service). The Bookshelf Review lists titles of new publications of interest to LIS professionals. Library Link Publishing Opportunities lists calls for conference papers, and invitations to contribute to electronic and hard-copy journals. There is also a section listing forthcoming conferences and exhibitions, workshops and discussion groups.

Free Pint
http://www.freepint.co.uk/
Free Pint is a weekly e-mail newsletter, produced by information professionals in the UK, which aims to provide guidance on more effective use of the web. Provides the latest IT news and answers your Internet research questions.

Web directories of library resources

You can find many directories and collections of resources that are related to library and information science on the web. There are not so many that are restricted to public libraries but many general LIS resources will have much to offer for the public library. The sites chosen here provide good starting points.

BUBL Link
http://www.bubl.ac.uk/link/l/
BUBL is an Internet-based information service produced for the UK higher education community. The BUBL catalogue of evaluated Internet resources contains many library-related links that will be of use to public libraries. The URL given here takes you to 'L' in the A–Z listing where you will find 24 library-related categories, ranging from 'Library catalogues in England' to 'Library Internet use'. Some categories of particular interest to the public librarian will be library and information science research, library and information science education, library and information science links, and library and information science news.

The UK Public Libraries Page

http://dspace.dial.pipex.com/town/square/ac940/ukpublib.html

It is probably not an exaggeration to say that this should be your first port of call when searching for UK public library information on the Internet. These frequently updated pages contain many useful links such as a listing of all UK and European public libraries on the web, links to professional organizations, information on policy-making and network strategy and library suppliers. Net Notions is a section well worth a look as it aims to provide ideas for small-scale networking initiatives that public libraries can develop.

Library and Related Resources

http://www.ex.ac.uk/library/wwwlibs.html

A straightforward listing, produced by the University of Exeter, of Internet resources that are provided by libraries, museums, research centres and publishers. Good selection of links to national libraries worldwide.

PICK: Quality Internet Resources in Library and Information Science

http://www.aber.ac.uk/~tplwww/e/

Resources selected by the Thomas Parry Library at the University of Wales Aberystwyth. The links are arranged in four categories that cover libraries and related organizations, LIS documents, librarianship and information science and use of networks.

US Public Libraries with Websites

http://www.capecod.net/epl/public.libraries.html

An A–Z listing, by state, of websites of US public libraries.

Librarians' Resource Centre: The Toolbox

http://www.sla.org/chapter/ctor/toolbox/resource/

The Toolbox is produced by the Special Libraries Association of Toronto. It is a wide-ranging collection of selected library and information retrieval resources. Section 1 focuses on public services and includes pointers to search engines, topical guides, ready reference and databases on the Net. Section 2 is devoted to professional development, knowledge management and library literature, while Section 3 covers technical services, providing guides, for example, for cataloguing, and Internet and intranet web page development tools.

COPAC

http://copac.ac.uk/copac/

COPAC gives access to the online catalogues of some of the largest university research libraries in the UK and Ireland with links to the web pages of each of the contributing libraries.

Library and information science journals

The online journals chosen for mention here do not focus exclusively on public libraries (there simply aren't many of these online yet); rather, they include the public sector in the wider context of the library and information community. As the web becomes more widely used in public libraries, it is likely that online publications devoted to the public sector will start appearing. A number of the journals included aim to provide a European and/or global perspective.

Ariadne
http://www.ariadne.ac.uk/
The main aim of this web-based magazine is to report on developments in UK higher education electronic library and information services. However, much is of interest to the wider library and information sector and there is a regular column devoted to public libraries.

Managing Information
http://www.aslib.co.uk/man-inf/
Free access to a selection of articles from this monthly journal produced by Aslib.

American Libraries Online
http://www.ala.org/alonline/
The magazine of the American Library Association. Includes regular columns on Internet topics and library technology, as well as the latest news and feature articles.

Exploit Interactive
http://www.exploit-lib.org/
This web-based journal, funded by the European Union, is designed to promote the results of EU library research projects, many of which involve public libraries.

Biblio Tech Review
http://www.biblio-tech.com/
This offers comment and analysis on the library automation industry. Useful

for keeping up to date with what's going on with commercial suppliers. Bibl Tech is a UK-based company.

LJDigital
http://www.ljdigital.com/
LJDigital is an electronic version of the US-published *Library Journal*. It con bines news, features and commentary with analyses of public polic technology and management developments and reviews. A selection of th journal's contents can be accessed free of charge.

Internet Resources Newsletter
http://www.hw.ac.uk/libWWW/irn/irn.html
This is a free monthly electronic newsletter, produced by Heriot-Wa University, publicizing new resources on the Internet. The emphasis is o engineering, science and social science resources, but it includes plenty of othe subjects. There is a section that reviews Internet publications in print forn each month 'Nice' websites are highlighted and given longer reviews. Of th sites included *PINAKES* is perhaps worth a special mention as this links to number of major subject gateways, from the *The WWW Virtual Library* tha covers all subject areas, to specific gateways such as *SOSIG* for social scienc and *GEM* for educational resources.

D-Lib Magazine
http://www.dlib.org/
The magazine is produced monthly and aims to support the development o the digital library. This is a US-based initiative with a global perspective. Th site is mirrored in the UK by UKOLN (at **http://mirrored.ukoln.ac.uk/lis journals/dlib/dlib/**).

Katherine Sharp Review
http://www.lis.uiuc.edu/review/
A peer-reviewed web journal devoted to research within library and informa tion science. A US-based magazine with the site being mirrored in the UK b UKOLN (at **http://mirrored.ukoln.ac.uk/lis-journals/review/**).

Library and Information Management Online
http://www.liblink.co.uk/limo/
Free online journal produced by Library Link, with a global perspective.

unding

he major national sources of funding for public libraries in the UK are currntly the New Opportunities Fund (NOF) and the European Commission. nce it has only recently been launched, information about *nof-digitize* is only adually being made available online. However, you will find a wealth of formation about the EC's funding programmes in general, though knowing here to start can be a problem. The sites suggested below try to provide a connient starting-point.

People's Network Online
http://www.lic.gov.uk/pno/
he official website of the People's Network project. Background information the initiative is available and the site aims to track the implementation of CT developments in public libraries using statistical data on *NETbase*. There a useful collection of related links and examples of services that demonstrate naginative use of ICT.

New Library Ideas Bank
http://www.earl.org.uk/ideabank/
n initiative from EARL that aims to bring together information on the development of *New Library* content. The site provides a forum for discussion and aring of ideas. There is background information on the People's Network, formation about digital content creation and management, plus links to amples of electronic content services that are already up and running, and OF funding opportunities.

New Opportunities Fund
http://www.nof.org.uk/
or information about the Fund and its grant programmes.

nof.digitise.org
http://www.nof.org.uk/tempdigit/index.html
Vebsite for the NOF digitization programme. The site is still being developed the moment, but in time will link to all the web-based projects that are nded through this programme. The site is intended to become a comprehenve directory of all NOF-supported digital information and material. uidance notes and an application form can be downloaded from the site.

Resource
http://www.resource.gov.uk/
The Library and Information Commission provided funding for librar research. Resource have now replaced the LIC and details of their grant should be available on their website. In the meantime, information about LI(grants is still available at **http://www.lic.gov.uk/grants/**.

The European Commission's Information Society Technologies Website
http://www.cordis.lu/ist/
The IST programme is the funding programme with most relevance to publi libraries and this site is intended to be a gateway for primary information o this programme. It provides information for those intending to prepare a pro posal, and provides information on IST projects already active. A section i devoted to providing help in finding potentially suitable project partners.

Cultural Heritage and EC funding
http://inf2.pira.co.uk/pub/ecwebsite97.html
This site, independent of the European Commission, is designed to explain i simple terms the EC funding process, focusing on the programmes open t museums, archives and libraries. The site includes background informatio about the various programmes, timescales of calls and a very useful section o the mechanics of the bidding process.

DCMS/Wolfson Public Libraries Challenge Fund
http://www.culture.gov.uk/heritage/
Information about the current call and the background of the Fund is availabl from the libraries section of the DCMS website.

Career development

This section highlights websites providing aspects of training and professiona development information and job vacancies. The Internet can be a very usefu tool in job-hunting as many (worldwide) opportunities can be easily accesse and frequently checked.

Training

LA Training and Development
http://www.la-hq.org.uk/directory/training-dev.html

A list of the training and development courses that are available from the Library Association.

LA Careers and Qualifications
http://www.la-hq.org.uk/directory/careers/where.html
Information about LIS qualifications and contact details for all UK institutions running postgraduate and undergraduate LIS courses. Includes information about qualifications available for library assistants.

AslibTtraining
http://www.aslib.co.uk/training/
List of training courses and seminars run by Aslib.

LISSPS
http://hosted.ukoln.ac.uk/lissps/
Website for the mailing list for library and information studies students and prospective students.

OWL: The Oxford Website for Library Trainees
http://www.lib.ox.ac.uk/owl/
This website is designed for those thinking of an LIS career, as well as current library trainees. Although the site is run by trainees in Oxford academic libraries, there is a section on public libraries which includes job descriptions from staff working in public libraries, information about library schools, funding and general library-related links.

The Lipstick Librarian
http://www.teleport.com/~petlin/liplib/
A humorous site devoted to changing the public perception of the librarian!

Job-hunting

LIBEX – the Bureau for International Library Staff Exchange
http://www.aber.ac.uk/~tplwww/libex.html
This is a free service and helps in arranging job exchanges with LIS professionals in other countries. Applicants post details of their current position and the type of post with which they want to exchange. Apart from the UK, the most popular countries for exchange at the present time are Australia and the USA.

LA JobNet

http://www.la-hq.org.uk/directory/job_seeking/jobnet.html

The online version of the Library Association's *Library and Information Appointments* which is published every fortnight. With the exception of the local press, this is the major source of public library vacancies. Allows searching by location and sector.

ALA Employment

http://www.ala.org/education/

From here you can link to vacancies published by the American Library Association. Postings are updated daily.

IFLANET: LIBJOBS

http://www.ifla.org/II/lists/libjobs.htm

IFLA operates a moderated mailing list for international employment opportunities. You need to subscribe to receive postings, but the archives of posting can be viewed without subscribing. Although the list operates worldwide, it tends to be US dominated.

Prospects

http://www.aslib.co.uk/prospects/vacancies.html

Aslib's online vacancy service, providing a short list of UK vacancies.

Library Link Careers

http://www.liblink.co.uk/management/careers.html

US-dominated vacancies listing in the library and information management sector. Perhaps of more general interest is an archive of position papers on career-related issues.

PART 3

Integrating the Internet into public library services

22

Producing web pages

- What makes a good public library website?
- Writing your library website
  - HTML
  - Web authoring tools
  - Java, Java Script and plug-ins
  - Design tips

This chapter explores the issues involved in developing public library websites, the basic skills needed, the principles of good design and the range of tools available for developing these sites.

What makes a good public library website?

A visit to the *UK Public Libraries Page* (**http://dspace.dial.pipex.com/town/square/ac940/ukpublib.html**) (which provides links to over 134 UK public library websites in the UK) shows the range in style, content and usefulness of public library websites. Like the proverbial little girl, when they're good they're very, very good and when they're bad they're horrid.

Some sites consist of a single page with information about opening hours and a picture of the Chief Librarian. In comparison, other sites provide access to the library catalogue, online reading groups, community information and e-mail reference services. Some sites are well designed and easy to navigate, whilst others are poorly presented, hard to use and badly out of date. This range in quality and ambition will be dependent upon a number of factors: the skills of the staff responsible for the site, the library's vision for its website and resources available for developing it.

There are a number of core elements which make a good public library website:

- ★ basic information
- ★ information about access to services
- ★ information about news and events
- ★ information about policies
- ★ web guide.

Basic information

Even the fanciest site should remember to provide somewhere core information about the library service. Opening hours and addresses may be dull, but users still often need this information.

Access to services

Libraries should aim to make as many of their services as possible available through their site. Initially this may mean putting the library catalogue and the community information database online. More ambitious ideas are discussed in Chapter 23.

Suffolk County Council has made its catalogue available on its website. Library users can remotely search the catalogue, renew books and make reservations:

http://libcat.suffolkcc.gov.uk/

Hertfordshire County Council Library Services has made its community information system available online and accessible from its library home page:

http://hertslib.hertscc.gov.uk/

The Enoch Pratt Free Library provides its patrons with remote access to its CD-ROMS and online databases:

http://www.pratt.lib.md.us/databases/

News and events

A good public library site will be continually updated with information about events, exhibitions and other news about library services. The website should be used as the means for providing users with the latest information about library services. The library website could also provide information about things like book prizes, poetry competitions and national library initiatives.

Kingston Libraries make library news a feature of their home page:

http://www.kingston.gov.uk/libs/

Policies

Libraries should make information about all their public polices available on their website. North Lincolnshire Libraries have a link to their library plan from their home page:

http://www.northlincs.gov.uk/library/

Manchester Libraries make information about their acceptable use of Internet services available online:

http://www.manchester.gov.uk/mccdlt/docs/networks/policy.htm

Web guide

Many public library websites contain a collection of links for their users. These collections point to high-quality Internet resources which the library believes may be of interest to its users. These collections become an online reference library. Web guides could point to resources which are relevant for particular departments within the library, for example, children, local history and business resources. The development of these collections is discussed in Chapter 23.

North Lincolnshire Library have a useful collection of national and local links:

http://www.northlincs.gov.uk/library/links.htm

Other services

Increasingly the library website will become the doorway to online versions of current and new services. There is real scope for libraries to develop online services which will open up access to their existing core services – ideas for these services are discussed in Chapter 23.

Writing your library website

In order to develop your library website you need to have a basic understanding of HTML (HyperText Markup Language) and website design. This section aims to provide a basic introduction to this topic. It will not teach you how to write web pages, but it will tell you where can find the necessary information to learn how to.

Learning HTML

HTML is the mark-up language which is used to write web pages. Mark-up languages instruct computers how to display text and how, to some degree, to format it. HTML is actually very simple and the basics can be learnt very quickly. There are a large number of freely available HTML tutorials available on the web. There are also numerous books on the topic and most local colleges run courses on learning to write web pages.

Online HTML tutorials

HTML Wizards: Tutorials
http://www.htmlwizards.com/

Writing HTML
http://www.mcli.dist.maricopa.edu/tut/

Guides to Writing HTML Documents
http://www.hypernews.org/HyperNews/get/www/html/guides.html
A directory of useful resources.

HTML: an interactive tutorial for beginners
http://www.davesite.com/webstation/html/

Web authoring tools

When the web initially developed, people wrote web pages 'by hand' – they used a simple text editor like Notepad or Wordpad and typed in the necessary HTML codes themselves. This meant that you had to know HTML codes and understand how they worked in order to develop pages. In the last five years, web authoring tools have developed and made web page authoring simpler.

They allow you to produce high-quality web pages and sites with little knowledge of HTML. Most web authoring tools look like word-processors, allowing you to write pages as you would in a word-processor. All the HTML is done behind the scenes by the authoring tool.

Web authoring tools allow the user:

- ★ to be confident that they have used valid HTML
- ★ to develop more ambitious pages very easily
- ★ to manage and maintain their website (FrontPage, for example, will check for broken links and automatically update internal links if a file is moved).

When choosing a web authoring tool it may be wise to consult with your council IT department and find out which are compatible with the server which will make the pages available to web browsers. FrontPage, for example, requires a set of software extensions to be installed on the server before some of its more advanced features can be used. More information about particular web authoring tools can be found below.

PC Magazine Online Web Authoring Tools Reviews
http://www.zdnet.com/pcmag/features/htmlauthor/_open.htm

FrontPage
http://www.microsoft.com/frontpage/

HotMetal
http://www.hotmetalpro.com/

HotDog
http://www.sausage.com/

HTML Assistant Pro
http://www.exit0.com/

Macromedia Dreamweaver
http://www.macromedia.com/software/dreamweaver/

Homesite
http://www2.allaire.com/Products/HomeSite/

NetObject Fusion
http://www.netobjects.com/

Visual Page
http://www.symantec.com/region/uk/product/vpage/fs_vpwin20.html

Adobe Pagemill
http://www.adobe.com/products/pagemill/

GoLive
http://www.adobe.com/products/golive/main.html

Java, JavaScript and all that plug-in jazz

Java and JavaScript are two programming languages that can be used to enhance the interactivity and dynamic features of a web page. They can be used to perform calculations, check forms and write interactive games and other interactive features. Java is a more complicated language than JavaScript (and yes, they're not the same thing). Again, there are many tutorials available on the web which teach how to develop Java and JavaScript resources. Also available are Java and JavaScript resources which have been already developed by someone else and which can be incorporated into pages free of charge.

Plug-ins are additional pieces of software that can be used to augment web browsers. Shockwave, Flash and Real Audio are three of the plug-ins which are most commonly encountered. Shockwave and Flash allow the browser to show multimedia resources – movies, games, animations. RealAudio allows the browser to play video and sound resources in real time (compared with having to download all of a file before it can be played). The real-time aspect of RealAudio means that it is possible to listen and view live events, eg all Radio One programmes can be listened to in real time via the Internet using the RealAudio plug-in.

The Java Tutorial
http://java.sun.com/docs/books/tutorial/

Java Coffee Break
http://www.javacoffeebreak.com/

Thau's Javascript Tutorial
http://hotwired.lycos.com/webmonkey/javascript/tutorials/tutorial1.html ?tw=javascript

JavaScript at Webdeveloper
http://www.webdeveloper.com/javascript/

Browser Plug-ins
http://www.netscape.com/plugins/index.html

Real Audio
http://www.realaudio.com/

Flash
http://www.macromedia.com/software/flash/

Shockwave
http://www.shockwave.com/

Technical terms glossaries

Yahoo! provides a good collection of links to Internet glossaries – so if you do get confused between Java and JavaScript, plug-ins and POPs, this will help make it all clear.

Internet Glossaries at Yahoo!
http://uk.dir.yahoo.com/Computers_and_Internet/Internet/Information_and_Documentation/Internet_Glossaries/

Netlingo: The Internet Language Dictionary
http://www.netlingo.com/
A useful technical glossary.

Basic good web design tips

All web pages, no matter what their content, should conform to some basic good design rules. Again, there are plenty of resources available on the Internet which provide guidance about what constitutes good web design. The list of design tips below summarizes much of this guidance.

Accessibility

The Internet is a significant development for people who are blind or partially sighted. The Royal National Institute for the Blind identifies the Internet as important because

> For the first time, many blind and partially sighted people have access to the same wealth of information as sighted people and on the same terms. A blind Net user in the United Kingdom (or indeed anywhere in the world) can now read today's issue of *The Times*, can locate the best restaurants in Paris or search records in the Library of Congress, in exactly the same way as a sighted person might. All it takes is accessible *Website design* and the right equipment.
>
> **http://www.rnib.org.uk/rnib/about.htm**

Many blind or partially sighted people may use a text reader to access the web. A text reader is a piece of software which reads web pages aloud. Text readers rely on web pages following a few basic design rules. If these rules have not been followed, then that page will be inaccessible to anyone who is using a text reader. Internet browsers also provide the user with the option to increase font size and control the way in which they view the website. Website design, therefore, needs to include enough flexibility so that users who are accessing and reading the site in different ways can still make use of it.

The World Wide Web Consortium (W3C) has been working on producing simple guidelines for website designers which, if followed, will ensure that their sites are as accessible as possible. Their checklist at (**http://www.w3.org/TR/WAI-WEBCONTENT/full-checklist**) allows you to assess just how accessible your site is and how it can be made more accessible.

WAI Quick Tips Reference Card
http://www.w3.org/WAI/References/QuickTips/
The *Quick Tips Reference Card* provides a dozen tips about how to design accessible websites. These tips can be printed out as a leaflet or can be reproduced as business card-sized reminders.

The Royal National Institute for the Blind (RNIB) also provides a number of resources about designing accessible websites.

Hints for Designing Accessible Websites
http://www.rnib.org.uk/wedo/research/hints.htm
A useful selection of top tips from the RNIB.

Can Everyone Read your Website?
http://www.rnib.org.uk/wedo/training/audit.htm
The RNIB offers an audit service where they will assess just how accessible your website really is.

Bobby
http://www.cast.org/bobby/
Bobby is a very useful tool for checking immediately how accessible your web pages are. You simply enter the web address of your pages and *Bobby* brings back an almost immediate report about how accessible it is. This is a free service and is very simple to use.

Disabled Accessibility – the Pragmatic Approach
http://www.useit.com/alertbox/990613.html
A useful discussion of how to ensure your web pages are accessible, by Jakob Nielsen.

Aim of the design

It is essential that you consider the impression that you are trying to create with your website before you start thinking about design. How important is it that it has an impressive, 'designer' look? Does it need to follow the corporate identity of your local authority or is a simply designed, easy-to-use site that doesn't need of a lot of plug-ins and advanced technologies your priority? Don't design for design's sake!

Metadata

This aids the identification, description and location of networked resources. Metadata tags describing various parts of the data held on a web page, such as the creator, title and language, are embedded into the HTML of the page. Resources that contain metadata can be searched and indexed in increasingly sophisticated ways.

Metadata Information
http://www.ukoln.ac.uk/metadata/

Contact details

How easy is it for someone using your website to find the contact details of the website manager or your organization? All too often contact details are overlooked, leaving the website user without the means to contact the organization. Having a contact e-mail address at the bottom of each page makes this process a lot easier. It is also good practice to include information on each page about when it was last updated.

Navigation

You may need to take a step back and consider how intuitive your site is to navigate for someone not familiar with how the library (or council) is organized. Traditional organizational structures which work well for managing your physical resources, such as staff and book stock, may not work as well when translated to your virtual library.

Download time

The length of time it takes a page to download is a major factor in its usability. Someone accessing a site from a slow modem at home is unlikely to wait five or ten minutes for a page to download. Faster access can be provided by avoiding large and unnecessary graphics. Some web editing tools will tell you how long your site will take to download.

Whistles and bells

Before incorporating something whizzy into your site like Flash or Shockwave you need to consider why you're using it. Did you just animate your logo because it would look nice? Is there a practical purpose for including web pages which will require your user to download another piece of software so they can access them? Make sure that plug-ins are only used when they're necessary – a game for children for example, a sound recording of someone speaking – and always make sure that a non-plug-in version is available. One of the worst design faults is to have a home page with a zippy Flash animation on it with no non-Flash alternative – people without Flash are likely to venture no further into your site and go somewhere else.

Audience

As with the development of all services, consider your audience. Is your website aiming to reflect all your current library services (and more) or are you at the early stages of website development and have perhaps decided to provide a web presence for a particular area, such as local history only? User surveys can be useful in finding out what people want, but be aware that users with little web experience may have low expectations.

Designing for the web not the leaflet

The web is an interactive, non-linear medium so ensure that your website makes the most of its interactive features.

General information about good web design can be found at the resources listed below. Of particular interest will be the UK Government's guidelines for government websites. These guidelines provide information about the minimum standards required for all government websites.

Government framework policy and guidelines for public sector websites
http://www.iagchampions.gov.uk/guidelines/websites/websites.html

Good Style Guidelines
http://www.earl.org.uk/taskgroups/policy/
Forthcoming issue paper from the UKOLN/EARL/ LA Networked Services Policy Taskgroup.

Web Design Tips
http://www.colin.mackenzie.org/webdesign/

Web Pages that Suck
http://www.webpagesthatsuck.com/

Alertbox: Jacob Nielsen's Column on Web Usability
http://www.useit.com/alertbox/

23

Developing online public library services

- ★ What is an online service?
- ★ The online public library
- ★ Service ideas
- ★ Issues

The Internet allows the public library both to access information and services online, and also to make their own services and information available online. Such online services will make available library resources and services 24 hours a day, seven days a week. Library services will no longer be tied to the opening hours of the library building. This chapter is intended to be an introduction to the issues involved in developing such online public library services. It is intended to provide ideas and food for thought – but not to be definitive. There is no one way of developing online local public library services – the level, range and purpose of these services will depend on the aims of each individual library.

What is an online service?

An online service is one which can be accessed via the Internet, typically via a website. The service will probably be available 24 hours a day and may be completely automated. Examples of online services include the Railtrack railway timetable (**http://www.railtrack.co.uk/travel/**), Amazon (**http://www.amazon.co.uk/**), NHS Direct (**http://www.nhsdirect.nhs.uk/**) and Easyjet (**http://www.easyjet.com/**).

The benefits of online services to users are:

24-hour access
access from the user's desktop (no need to visit a physical service-point)
there is potentially more accessibility for people with disabilities
services can be tailored to the user's specific needs
no need to queue!

enefits of providing online services for the service provider are:

- the automation of staff-intensive tasks
- having a service-point open 24 hours a day
- being able to deliver a service directly into the user's home
- being able to tailor services quickly to meet individual user's needs
- being able to reach more users.

n online service allows the user the freedom to deal with the service provider hen and where they wish to. It allows the service provider the opportunity to each a greater audience, to free itself from office hours and to adapt its services match more closely the needs of its users.

he online public library

ibraries currently operate within fixed opening hours and via physical serice-points. These opening hours and locations may not map on to the needs f their users. For some users the nearest library may simply be too far away to isit, or shut when they have free time. By developing online services libraries ave the opportunity to make themselves more available. An online service will e available at 3am to the nurse who has finished his shift, it will be available the crofter who lives 80 miles from the nearest library, it will be available to he home learners, children in classrooms and the housebound. The developnent of online services provides an opportunity to reach people, via a omputer, who currently do not or cannot access library services.

The development of content-rich online services is being undertaken by all orts of organizations. Shops, entertainment providers, financial services and ducators are all beginning to provide Internet-accessible services. If libraries on't develop their own online services they are in danger of being left behind.

Service ideas

Ideas for possible online public library services are discussed in this sectio This is not intended to be a definitive list, but simply a starting-point for idea Where possible, examples of libraries already providing similar online servic are given. All these ideas are firmly rooted in the traditional service aims of tl public library community.

A useful starting-point for ideas for integrating the Internet into publ library services is the list of *Innovative Internet Applications in Libraries* mai tained by Kathy Leeds at Wilton Library, USA:

http://www.wiltonlibrary.org/innovate.html

Children's services

The Internet can be used to enhance and complement current children's se vices in a number of ways.

Homework help

Internet links of interest to children can be collected together and presented i an easy-to-use index. If a number of libraries work together, a large and ver exhaustive index can be created. Resources listed in this online index woul carry the librarian's stamp of approval and could act as an online virtual chi dren's collection.

The American Library Association has already developed an Interne resource guide to 700 great sites for kids. *Kids Click!* is an even more sophisti cated example of this type of service. This is a proactive online service whic fulfils the library's traditional role of providing access to quality resources.

ALA Great Sites for Kids
http://www.ala.org/parentspage/greatsites/

Kids Click!
http://sunsite.berkeley.edu/KidsClick!/

Individual libraries have also developed pointers for Internet resources for thei child users.

South Ayrshire Libraries
http://www.south-ayrshire.gov.uk/libraries/coolsites.htm

Boston Public Library Homework Help
http://www.bpl.org/WWW/KIDS/HomeworkHelp.html

omework help can also be provided via e-mail. Children could e-mail in eir reference queries to the library instead of having to visit. Again, this is a rvice which may work more effectively with libraries working in partnership. he American Library Association already provides a similar service called idsConnect:
http://www.ala.org/ICONN/AskKC.html

romoting reading online

he use of the Internet to promote reading has been successfully demonstrated y the Stories from the Web project. At the heart of this UK public library project is a website which provides access to snippets and extracts of current ildren's literature. The aim of these extracts is to intrigue and interest the ild so that they seek out the book and read it. A range of online activities cused around each story are also available, which further seek to encourage e child to imaginatively interact with the story. In addition to the website, ubs are being run in the three libraries across the UK where children follow a rogramme of centrally devised activities. These activities are typically focused round something on the website, but use story-telling sessions, story writing, uthor visits, etc to bring these stories to life.

Stories from the Web
http://hosted.ukoln.ac.uk/stories/

xamples of other innovative children's library services are:

East Sussex Libraries provide online games for their users:
http://www.eastsussexcc.gov.uk/lia1/kidsonline/games/arcade.htm

Iultnomah County Libraries children's web pages give news about events in he library, tied in to calendar events, and even provide a monthly library joke:
http://www.multnomah.lib.or.us/lib/kids/index.html

n easy resource to make available on a website is a list of recommended books. With very little further effort these lists can be linked in to reviews fro children themselves.

New York Public Library Recommended Reads
http://www.nypl.org/branch/kids/lists.html

Berkeley Teen Reads
http://www.infopeople.org/bpl/teen/reviews.html

Conwy Wicked Books
http://www.conwy.gov.uk/english/2council/library_information_archive kidzone/wickedbooks/Ec3.html

Adult reader development

Reader development is a service area which has gained particular attention recent years. Initiatives like Well Worth Reading and the DCMS Read Development Challenge Fund have helped reader development services public libraries in the UK. There is great potential for developing these servic online too.

Book groups

A traditional library-run book group has to meet in a certain place at a certai time – for people who only have free time when the library is shut or don't li near a library these groups are not accessible. An online book group, howeve is accessible to anyone with Internet access. Using e-mail, members of th online group can share their ideas and reactions to a book with each othe Group members are able to collect and read their e-mail at a time convenie to them. The discussion may be led by a group leader who will post questior and comments to the list and set the ground rules for the discussion.

Many examples of online book groups already exist, although few have bee developed by libraries. If a library wishes to run an online book group it wi need to promote the list, invest in some software to run it and assign someon the role of administering the list and leading the discussion.

The Book Group List
http://books.rpmdp.com/

Bookwire List of Online Book Groups
http://www.bookwire.com/index/reading-groups.html

Baltimore County Public Library – a library-run list!
http://www.bcplonline.org/centers/library/bookclub.html

The development of online library reader development services is interesting when compared with the development of the huge online bookshops like *Amazon*, *Bol* and *WHSmith online*. There is much that libraries can learn about promoting reading online from these organizations. Unlike libraries, they are solely dependent on their ability to promote their stock in an online environment in order to survive. Although some of their sales may come from people seeking to buy a particular book, many of their sales come from browsers – people who want something to read but don't know what exactly. In order to help the browsers make a book selection, the bookshops have had to develop means to promote their stock online.

The online bookshops' answer to this problem has been two-fold. Obviously each shop needs to have a catalogue so the customer can discover what books are for sale. However, traditional catalogues are not effective promotion tools – they tell the user what books are in stock, but don't provide any information about the book other than basic bibliographic details. There is no cover photograph, no synopsis of the plot, no comments from critics and no opportunity to read the first (or last!) page of the book to gain an idea of its writing style. Catalogues of this kind are only useful for the customer who is searching for a specific book.

The online bookshops have resolved these issues by giving their catalogues added value. In addition to basic bibliographic details, their catalogues provide an image of the front cover, a synopsis and, often, critical reviews. They also generally allow their users to add their own reviews to the catalogue record of each book. In this way the browser can find out what other readers thought of the book and gain a kind of personal recommendation. The bookshops have transformed their catalogues from book location tools to book promotion tools.

Amazon.co.uk
http://www.amazon.co.uk/

BOL uk
http://www.uk.bol.com/

Internet Bookshop
http://www.bookshop.co.uk/

Library catalogues are purely functional in comparison. Initially developed for use by the librarian rather than the reader, they provide no more than the bibliographical details of each item in the collection. There is obvious scope for libraries to develop their catalogues in the same way as online bookshops. A richer, more informative catalogue would transform the book selection process of a house-bound reader. Rather than being dependent on the choices of books made for them by library staff, they would be able to actively make informed decisions by browsing the catalogue itself. For the user who has only a few minutes spare to visit the library building, an informed book selection process can be made beforehand using the catalogue. The mobile library service could also be transformed. No longer dependent on just browsing the stock in the mobile library, users could meaningfully interact with the catalogue and make informed book selection choices for themselves – the mobile library would deliver the items the following week.

Catalogue data could also be made to work harder – again following the example of the online bookshops. Reader profiles could be developed by tracking what library users borrow from the library. The catalogue itself could suggest books to borrow to readers based on the book-borrowing patterns of other readers. Readers could also be asked to rate the books they borrow, allowing the library to build up effective profiles. Readers could choose or not choose to participate in these schemes, as they wished, and careful data protection procedures would need to be put in place.

Internet Bookshop has Jenny the Online Librarian to help recommend books to you:

http://www.bookshop.co.uk/jen/jenpge.asp

Amazon's Recommendation Service
http://www.amazon.co.uk/exec/obidos/subst/delivers/delivers-signup.html/

E-mail can be used to inform users with online access when new books become available in the library. The library can use e-mail to deliver monthly bulletins about new stock to its users for very little cost. The library website can be used to highlight and promote sections of stock, online exhibitions can be developed on particular topic areas, and author interviews and online chats can also be made available. Some of these services may be more effectively developed in collaboration with other libraries.

(Es)senses of Place
http://www.cam.net.uk/home/var/essenses/
This is an example of an online exhibition developed by Cambridgeshire Library Service for the 1997 National Library Week.

Reference

The Internet is a fantastic reference tool. It makes available a mind-boggling mass of information from around the world. Providing meaningful access to these resources is one of the main challenges for libraries. The library user is going to need guidance from the library in finding the best online resource for their information need. They may also need guidance in realizing that their query can still be most easily answered using a book!

One way of helping users find what they want on the Internet is to develop an online collection of links. Many libraries have already been doing this. These collections are available via the library's website and act as virtual reference collections.

It should be noted that as many organizations have already developed extensive collections of reference links it may be more time-effective for libraries simply to point to these collections rather than developing their own. Individual libraries, though, will be able to develop useful pages of local links for their users.

Internet Public Library Ready Reference Collection
http://www.ipl.org/ref/RR/

EARLweb
http://www.earl.org.uk/earlweb/

North Lincolnshire Libraries – Local Links
http://www.northlincs.gov.uk/library/loclinks.htm

Some users may still require a librarian to find the answer to their reference question for them. Traditionally the library user visits the library, queues at the reference desk and eventually gets to ask their question. (Alternatively the user may ring the library.) In both cases the reference interview takes place in real time and the user expects to receive their answer immediately. This system works reasonably well assuming that the query is not time-consuming or complicated. As most reference queries are received at peak times, lunch time and early evening, dealing with a complicated query can lengthen the queue, put additional pressure on busy staff and generally be unsatisfactory for staff and user alike. Some of this burden could be shifted by developing e-mail-based reference services.

Libraries can encourage users with Internet access to e-mail their reference queries. Queries that arrive via e-mail can be answered when the library is quiet or shut! Queries can be routed to different libraries or answered by one central reference team. By allowing users to e-mail their queries, pressure will be lifted from the frontline reference desk. Users who still require an immediate answer to their query will continue to phone or visit in person, but others who can wait may find it more convenient to use e-mail.

Many libraries already provide an e-mail reference service and their experience suggests that it can be easily integrated into existing reference services. Questions can be asked either through a web-based form on the library website or simply via an e-mail address.

Essex Ask Us
http://www.essexcc.gov.uk/infoserv/ecc_lib/ask_us/ask_us.htm

Ask Your Library
http://www.conwy.gov.uk/english/2council/library_information_archives/askyourlib/Ec3.html

As with many online services there is potential for libraries to develop these services in collaboration with other libraries. *Ask a Librarian* is an excellent example of the kind of model that could be used. A central web page provides a form for users to submit their reference questions. These questions are then forwarded on to a reference library to answer. Reference libraries around the UK answer the queries using a rota system. This means that no one library is overloaded with enquiries.

Ask a Librarian
http://www.earl.org.uk/ask/

Ask a Librarian also maintains a list of frequently asked questions which allows the enquirer to check whether their question has been asked before (and see what the answer is) before submitting their own enquiry.

CD-ROMs and databases

Providing access to reference CD-ROMs and online databases through a library website is already being done regularly in the academic community. Library users no longer have to visit the university library to access these electronic resources. They are available through the library's website and can be accessed from any desktop.

Although making CD-ROMs and databases accessible through a website is technically quite straightforward, the legal issues surrounding licensing and copyright make this a difficult service to provide. CD-ROM vendors and database creators currently charge different fees for their products according to the number of people who access them. Buying one copy of a newspaper index CD-ROM to run on a standalone PC is obviously cheaper than buying a licence to make it accessible via a network across all branch libraries in the authority. As the cost of the product is usually calculated on the number of people who will use it, there are interesting challenges in making these services available online while restricting access.

Potentially, by making such resources available through a web page, anyone with Internet access will be able to use it. Product vendors are obviously not going to agree to this. In order to negotiate a licence with the vendor the library will need to decide how many potential users of the product there might be and to find some mechanism to limit the use of that product to perhaps only its registered readers. Methods of limiting access to such resources and authenticating legitimate users need to be put into place. Work on this has been done in the higher education community in the UK using the ATHENS authentication protocol. At the moment work in the public library community in this area is still at an early stage of development, but no doubt will develop rapidly in the next few years.

Athens
http://www.athens.ac.uk/

Examples of online databases available at the University of Bath:
http://www.bath.ac.uk/Library/info/databases/a-z.html

Family/local history

Traditionally, items in the family/local history collection have been difficult to access because of their uniqueness and fragility. People researching local or family histories have needed to travel to where the resources were because of this uniqueness. The development of online services has the potential to make these resources available online and consequently accessible to a far greater number of people.

Family and local history collections have often been left behind in the development of electronic catalogues or even catalogues of any kind. Sometimes the only way to find out what is included in some collections may be to visit the library or record office to consult a card catalogue. Obviously, before effective online local and family history services can be developed, steps will need to be taken to address this issue. Only when comprehensive electronic catalogues are available will the full range of family and local history collections be known.

Familia lists family history collections and key resources held in authorities across the UK. At the time of writing it did not provide access to the resources themselves, though.

http://www.earl.org.uk/familia/

Digitization has more potential than just scanning local history photograph collections. The digitization of text-based documentation like directories, papers and parish records is equally important.

Leeds Local Studies Library includes a searchable photographic database and 1914–18 war absent voters:

http://www.leeds.gov.uk/library/services/locnfam.html

Suffolk's Roll of Honour is a searchable database of names from Suffolk's War Memorials:

http://www.suffolkcc.gov.uk/libraries_and_heritage/sro/roh/

Cheshire Wills is an index of all wills made between 1492 and 1857 held at the Cheshire Record Office:

http://www.fhsc.org.uk/wills/

See Chapter 11 for other examples.

Whenever any digitization is undertaken, it is important that suitable standards are followed. Individual digital items should have metadata to ensure that they are easily findable and do not become buried in an electronic version of the catalogueless record office. Standards will also be important to ensure that cross-searching is possible between digital archives. Useful work on developing standards on this topic is currently being undertaken by the National Preservation Office.

National Preservation Office
http://www.bl.uk/services/preservation

Z39.50 is a protocol allowing cross-searching between different systems:
http://www.ukoln.ac.uk/dlis/z3950/

Information about metadata can be found on the UKOLN website:
http://www.ukoln.ac.uk/metadata/

Items from the digital archives can be repackaged in different ways and made accessible to a wider audience. Although the family historian may only be interested in the parish records and whether their ancestor appeared in them, a less focused member of the public may be more interested in a general exhibition about life in their area in the Victorian age. This virtual exhibition could draw on material from the digital archive and contextualize it with stories, historical facts, images and interactivity. This again would make the resources held in libraries and archives accessible to a wider audience.

Knowsley Local History is an online exhibition about Knowsley:
http://history.knowsley.gov.uk/

Santa Cruz Public Library is an extensive collection of articles about major topics in Santa Cruz's history:
http://www.santacruzpl.org/history/

The development of a digital archive of resources also provides public libraries with a number of income-generation activities. By making their local history photograph collection available on the Internet, the library makes it accessible to a wider audience. Some members of that audience may wish to order copies of the photos they have viewed on the website. Libraries could sell prints of these images. Other potential income may come from organizations or individuals who wish to use some of the images in other material. Before generating income from any of their collections in this way, libraries will have to ensure that the proper copyright rules have been followed. The Networked Services Policy Taskgroup have produced an issue paper entitled *Copyright and the networked environment* which addresses this topic.

Networked Services Policy Taskgroup
http://www.earl.org.uk/taskgroups/policy/index.html

Community information

Libraries are usually at the heart of any local community. They provide important information services for that community, often keeping the only directory of local resources such as childcare facilities, doctors, exhibitions and local clubs. Many of these directories have already been made available in an electronic format through videotext. Videotext is a basic computer system which has a central database of information which can only be viewed on dedicated terminals. These terminals are usually positioned in prominent public locations such as the library, the town hall, the sports centre or community centres. Information is text based and has the appearance of teletext pages. No other computer services can be provided on these terminals.

With the development of the Internet, many authorities have used it to make their community information systems accessible. These systems can be searched through the library's website. These websites provide comprehensive information about the resources of that local community.

Buckinghamshire Community Information Online
http://www.buckscc.gov.uk/Clink1.htm

Cambridgeshire Community Information Database
http://www.camcnty.gov.uk/infosearch.html

Increasingly, these online videotext systems are in competition with a range of other locally focused material on the Internet. Commercial companies and, in particular, local newspapers have been working to develop similar comprehensive information services, but using web technology. This means that the pages of information are more graphical, more flexible and more comparable to other information on the Internet. At present, though, there is little sign of these resources matching the depth of information held by libraries.

Cambridge Citizen's Guide
http://www.thisiscambridge.com/

Aylesbury and the Vale
http://www.aylesburyvale.net/

One way in which libraries could develop their community information services is to move into a more web-based model. Instead of hosting a limited amount of information about a local club, the library could provide that club with web space on its server. Instead of the library having to maintain the club's entry in the database, the club itself designs, maintains and develops its own pages. This gives the club greater scope for providing information about itself and makes it easier for it to update its information.

There may be a considerable overhead of support costs as the library trains and provides advice to the group about developing web pages. Again, it is important that standards are followed so that a search mechanism can search effectively across the information pages of different organizations. There is potential in this model for income generation if the library hosts web pages for local companies and businesses.

Croydon Web Design Service
http://www.croydon.gov.uk/frame-webdesign.htm

To further promote community information on its website the library could provide a daily diary of events taking place in the area, host other important information services such as a virtual notice-board, perhaps an items for sale bulletin board. The library could use its website as a constantly changing community resource which people use to find out what is happening in their community.

Whats On in Croydon
http://www.croydon.gov.uk/whatson/default.asp

Issues

The development of online services is very exciting for public libraries. It will free the library service from its building and allow it to be available to members of the public 24 hours a day, seven days a week. However, as with all new ideas, there are a number of issues that need to be resolved before such services can be developed on a large scale.

The cost of developing a comprehensive online service for an individual library authority may seem prohibitive. Initially, online services will be in addition to the more traditional services already being provided. These new services will have to be funded on top of current services. This will of course be challenging for any library manager.

Another interesting issue is how the library reacts if its initially expensiv online services are used by readers outside of the library's catchment area. Th wonder of the Internet is that geographical location no longer matters. If library has spent part of its budget developing an online reading group o online reference question service, how will it react when this service is used b non-registered readers – or in other words non-local tax payers.

The skills of staff to develop these services is also another issue. Currentl most public library staff have limited IT skills. The implementation of th New Opportunities Fund (NOF) training fund in the UK will help addres this issue; however, even then training is only for basic IT skills. The library i going to have either to retrain some of its staff or start recruiting staff with ne skills. To produce an effective website will require the dedicated time of at leas one staff member. This time will have to be timetabled into someone's dutie and not simply added on to existing duties.

As more people gain access to the Internet and use it in their daily lives, th library's website may become some people's only access point to the librar The same level of care will need to be taken about its presentation, quality an currency as is dedicated to library buildings themselves. Initially the development of online services will be challenging, frustrating and occasionall difficult. However, in the long run libraries will provide more and more c their services online and adapt their structures, their funding and their aims t support and manage these new services.

24

Providing public Internet access

- Developing policies for running the service
- Deciding whether to charge for the service
- Training the service users

Providing public Internet access can be complicated and needs careful planning if it is to be implemented successfully. Libraries need to consider the three main issues listed above as they plan and develop their public access Internet services.

Acceptable use

It is vital that every library providing public Internet access has an acceptable use policy. Public libraries have developed policies for most aspects of their services. These range from whether people can eat in the library to what happens if a book is lost. It is surprising, therefore, how many library authorities provide Internet access without making fundamental acceptable use policy decisions.

What is an acceptable use policy?

An acceptable use policy (AUP) defines how Internet services may be used in the library. Typically AUPs cover topics such as pornography on the Internet, patrons using chat rooms and the legal responsibilities of the library when offering Internet services. They also ensure that when an Internet resource is misused staff are clear on how they must deal with this misuse.

What should be in an acceptable use policy?

An AUP should include statements on the following points:

- ★ Why the library provides Internet access. This will place the Internet ser vices in the context of the library's overall aims.
- ★ The type of material that can accessed on the Internet and the fact that th library authority is not responsible for this material.
- ★ Who can use the Internet workstations – is it just library card-holders or ca anyone use them?
- ★ The type of resources made accessible to users from the workstations. Fo example, can users access chat rooms or buy books online? Are they allowe to play online games or Internet access is restricted to study purposes only?
- ★ The way in which users are expected to behave. This is really the pornogra phy issue – what type of content in web pages is acceptable to be viewed i the library?
- ★ What happens to people if they break the rules? A policy cannot be imple mented unless there are penalties for people who break it. What is don with the person who keeps coming in and playing online games in contra vention of an AUP? Will s/he be banned from the library? Be told o repeatedly? Have her/his Internet access rights withdrawn?
- ★ Use of Internet workstations by children. Can children surf the web on thei own or do their parents have to be with them? Do their parents have to sig a form saying that they give their children permission to surf the web an that the library isn't responsible if they come across any dubious material?
- ★ The library's use or non-use of filtering software. Why does/doesn't th library use filtering software? How well does it work? Can the library guar antee that the filter blocks out all objectionable material?

It is important that the library makes users of their Internet services aware c the AUP if it is to be implemented successfully. The library should conside making users have to read and sign acceptance of the AUP before they ar allowed Internet privileges. Alternatively the text of the policy could be dis played prominently by all Internet workstations.

Other issues to be aware of include ensuring that the AUP is compatibl with the rest of the library's policies. If your library states in its mission state ment that it aims to provide free access to all information in all formats thi will be inconsistent with a policy decision to use filtering.

Many public libraries have published their AUPs on the Internet. •llections of AUPs can be found at:

Networked Policy Taskgroup Website
http://www.earl.org.uk/taskgroups/policy/

Public Library Internet Access policies
http://www.ci.oswego.or.us/library/poli.htm
ease note that these are American public library AUPs and may not be suitle for use in a UK/European environment.

KOLN has developed a small number of resources about AUPs as part of its ork about filtering software. The material that can be downloaded includes a llection of excerpts from UK public library policies organized into topics, eg ildren and the Internet. Also available is a small collection of policy breakers hese are possible scenarios which will test any policy.
http://www.ukoln.ac.uk/public/present/nag/

harging

he issue of whether access to the Internet should be charged for is one that s been resolved in different ways by different library authorities in the UK. me authorities view the Internet as part of their core services and provide it r free. Suffolk Library and Arts Service state that 'We want to promote and spire learning through access to the information and educational resources of e world wide web, free at the point of use in all our service points.' Other thorities view Internet access as an income-generating service in the same ay videos and cassettes are managed. There are no national policy guidelines this topic and the decision to charge is an individual authority one. In many ses the introduction of charges at an early stage of Internet access process (via dial-up connection) has meant that this policy continued once the library oved to a network set-up.

More information about charging and the issues surrounding it are available an issue paper called 'Charging and Internet Services' written by Ian Everall d Sarah Ormes. The paper is freely available on the Internet and can be und at:
http://www.earl.org.uk/taskgroups/policy/issue_papers/charging.htm

Although basic Internet access may become a standard free service, this w not mean that libraries cannot charge for value-added services. Bath Publ Library, for instance, provides completely free access to all library card-holde but charges for non-library card-holders to use its Internet services. In a ci with a large numbers of tourists wishing to e-mail home, this becomes a usef income-generation activity.

Training

Training is an interesting issue for public librarians. Many library staff ha found themselves in the position of training members of the public to use th Internet when they themselves have received no or little training. A comm complaint among librarians managing Internet workstations on a day-to-d basis is that their users know more than they do. Often Internet access h been bolted on to existing services with little or no time spent training sta This situation has arisen because of lack of resources and little staff relea time available for training. In many small libraries librarians simply cannot b spared to attend training courses.

With the development of the New Opportunities Funding training initiati there is now a UK strategy to ensure that all UK public librarians are trained have at least basic IT and networking skills. Every UK library authority h been allotted a training allowance by the fund to be used to train its staff. Sta will complete a training course which will provide them with the Europea Computer Driving Licence (an internationally recognized qualification). It probable that training may take place in association with a local further educa tion or training college. Whereas some staff will be trained to have bas computer skills, others will be trained to have more developed technical skills.

Further information about this training initiative is available at:
http://www.nof.org.uk/edutemp.cfm?content=edu-4

Training library users is another service that needs careful planning and deve opment. After the NOF initiative, all library staff should be able to quick train a user in how to use a mouse, surf the Internet and try and find the info mation they require. However, many users may have much more complicate Internet training needs. They may wish to be trained in how to use th Internet to research their family history, they may need help in completin online forms, taking part in online education courses and how to develop the vn HTML skills. There is therefore an issue about just how much training oraries are going to do. Does the library's responsibility to the training needs the user stop after they have been given basic skills? Does the library have e resources to provide any additional training? What are the basic skills that orarians should train users in?

One possible solution could be through the development of Internet train- g classes. If space is available and funding can be found, the library could evelop a whole series of Internet training classes. Training classes could focus n specific topics such as researching your family history, local history on the nternet, writing web pages, useful homework resources, literature resources n the Internet, and so on. Internet classes could also be targeted at specific oups of library users, eg women returning to work, senior citizens. These asses could be developed as a value-added service which could be income enerating.

Conclusion: What's next?

Introduction

So far we have been looking at Internet facilities and opportunities that publ libraries can currently benefit from. Looking to the future, it seems certain th the opportunities offered by the Internet and its pervasiveness in the lives of a of us can only increase, given that the development of ICT is being supporte throughout our society by the twin driving forces of government and the com mercial sector. The fact that the Internet is being used by such diverse sectio of society for such diverse reasons demonstrates its huge potential. Although is difficult to predict a long-term view of how society will integrate use of th Internet, looking at some current initiatives a picture does begin to emerge the shape of a future digital society, at least in the short term.

Trends in society

Exploiting the potential of ICT is integral to the UK Government's vision of modern society and the role of public libraries in the development of this soc ety is now clearly established, due in a large part to the *New library* initiative This influential report was published by the Library and Informatio Commission in 1997, coinciding with the election of New Labour to offic The report picked up on the Government's desire to harness the potential the Internet to improve the quality and efficiency of its services, to increas learning and educational opportunities throughout society and to tackle th problems of social exclusion. Initiatives such as *Modernising Government*[2] an *Our information age*[3] have outlined the Government's commitment to, fo example, deliver all Government services electronically by 2008 and to ensur that public services are available 24 hours a day, seven days a week where ther is a demand. The Government is also encouraging cross-sector initiatives an ensuring that policy is made and implemented in a more joined-up wa

:gardless of the organizational structure of government, a move exemplified ı the creation of Resource: the Council for Museums, Libraries and Archives. artnerships and opportunities for the public and the private sector to work ›gether to devise and deliver services are also being encouraged as a way of roviding services that an increasingly sophisticated and articulate public want.

Commercial organizations are certainly an equal if not more significant driing force in determining the shape of the future digital society. As more and ıore of us experience the convenience of online shopping and banking serices that are tailored to our own personal requirements, we will come to xpect the same standards from all services, regardless of whether they are elivered by the public or private sector.

As the amount of information that is available increases, so we are able to ıake more informed choices and take greater responsibility for our own ealth, education and financial provisions throughout our lives. Initiatives ıch as *NHS Direct*,[4] that offers an around-the-clock confidential medical dvice service, are being designed to provide information to enable people to ıake informed decisions about their own healthcare. And in the education ɔhere, the Government is developing learning accounts that allow individuals) decide for themselves where to spend credits on educational and learning pportunities.

Media organizations too, such as the BBC, are demonstrating that, far from eing a rival to traditional forms of broadcast, the integration of the Internet ıto traditional services can enhance and extend these services. The BBC Iistory 2000 campaign[5] is an example of where additional material and activies can be developed from themes that have been delivered to a wide audience, ırough television broadcasts in this case, and delivered to a probably smaller, ut more interested online audience. The merger in early 2000 of America)nline and Time Warner to form the first 'clicks and mortar' company, was een as important and logical since it brought together AOL's online skills and nternet entry-point with Times Warner's content and cable network infraructure.[6]

These examples demonstrate how the power of the Internet is being xploited in all sectors of society and the economy. We can expect that in the ıture services which fail to deliver the advantages of convenience and personlization of experience that online delivery can offer will come to be regarded s having little relevance to how an increasing number of us live our lives.

Initiatives towards the digital society

We now take a look now at some of the current initiatives both in the publi library sector and the wider community that will determine networking devel opments and the Internet's relationship with the public library in the first year of the 21st century.

At the time of writing, the initiative that has the potential to make the great est impact on public libraries is the *People's Network* project.[7] This places publi libraries at the centre of Government plans to deliver the benefits of lifelon learning to every citizen in the country. The project arose from *New Librar* and can be seen as the principal kick-start for those libraries that have previ ously hesitated to develop online services and an initiative for furthe development for those public libraries that are already committed to the inte gration of networked services. The project started life as the Public Librar Network, and its subsequent name change signifies the desire for it to be a uni fying force for public information and community involvement. A specific ain of the project is to link every public library in the UK to the Internet by 2002 The development of the network is being supported by the *New Opportunitie Fund*, a National Lottery distributor,[8] which is making £270 million availabl for the creation of community learning centres and grids. It is expected tha public libraries will work together with other learning and information organi zations to develop these. As part of this funding initiative the nof-digitizatio programme[9] has £50 million available to fund projects which will make infor mation available in a digital format.

The *National Grid for Learning*[10] is a government initiative to support life long learning. The website is envisaged as an entry-point for learning an educational opportunities. Public libraries are expected to contribute to thi Grid principally through the inclusion of the People's Network.

Changing expectations for service provision and working patterns have beer taken into account in the creation of the *24 Hour Museum*.[11] This project i being designed as the UK gateway to museums, galleries and heritage, the ide being that people do not have to physically visit museums or galleries durin their opening hours to benefit from the vast repositories of information an artefacts that they hold. The *24 hour museum* site contains information abou museum opening times, collections and access and is developing themed activ ities such as treasure hunts and trails.

The *UfI* initiative[12] is intended as a catalyst for open and distance learning It is significant as it will deliver using 'modern technologies . . . making learn ng available at a time and place to suit the learner, at home, in the workplace and through [*learndirect*, a] national network of learning centres'.

The *Heritage Lottery Fund*[13] distributes National Lottery funds with the aim of safeguarding and enhancing the heritage of the UK. Its *Access to Archives*[14] programme aims to create a virtual national archives service, bringing together information about the very rich but widely dispersed national archival heritage and making it available globally from one source via the world wide web.

In *A netful of jewels: new museums and the learning age*,[15] a report from the National Museum Directors' Conference of 1999, the museums' community have recognised the potential opportunities for creating digital content from the treasures that they hold and the potential role that they have in the learning society and the creative economy.

Digital heritage and cultural content is one of the five main areas for research and technological development of the *European Commission's Information Society Technologies* programme.[16] The programme focuses on projects that aim to integrate access to materials in libraries, museums and archives, improve the operational efficiency of content holdings, and address preservation and access issues of multimedia content.

The shift towards the digital age is more marked in higher (and further) education libraries. This sector has benefited from a number of large-scale national and international programmes. The *Electronic Libraries Programme* (*eLib*)[17] was initiated in 1995 and has produced a body of projects aimed at 'engaging the Higher Education community in developing and shaping the implementation of the electronic library'. The programme is in its third phase, and is focusing on hybrid libraries (which incorporate electronic as well as print resources), large-scale resource discovery projects and digital preservation. A feature of the programme has been the development of a number of subject gateways that provide mediated access to evaluated network resources in specific subject areas. Subject gateways developed in this way include *SOSIG*[18] for the social sciences, *ADAM*[19] for art, design, architecture and media and *OMNI*[20] for medical information. The *Resource Discovery Network*[21] is aiming to bring a number of these subject gateways or 'hubs' together to create a significant resource, offering, for example, the opportunity to search for information across several hubs at the same time.

The *Distributed National Electronic Resource* (*DNER*)[22] is a managed environment for accessing quality-assured information resources on the Internet which are available from many sources. The resources include journals, monographs, textbooks, abstracts, manuscripts, maps, music scores, still images an geospatial images and other numeric data, as well as moving picture and soun collections. This is a nationally coordinated JISC initiative for the higher edu cation community. The aim is to provide an electronic resource which appear seamless to the user (unlike current electronic services where different service require different search techniques). Available through the HE communit network JANET, staff and students will be able to access resources effectivel and efficiently through intuitive and customized interfaces.

The *DCMS/Wolfson Public Libraries Challenge Fund*[23] was established in Jul 1997 to enhance the services and facilities provided by public libraries i England. Calls for proposals are issued annually with the DCMS contributin £2 million a year and the Wolfson Foundation £1 million a year. The fund ha previously supported projects that will establish new, or develop existing, I' network facilities in public libraries in England. The focus now is on the devel opment of content to be delivered over the network infrastructure.

Future services influenced by social and economic trends

The digital age means many things to many people. The Internet will be use (and abused) in all sorts of ways for all sorts of reasons. However, commo themes do emerge from the way in which networking is being exploited by th Government and the public and private sector.

Collaboration, both geographically and across sectors in a networked envi ronment, is not only possible but desirable. Joining together and sharin information reduces the duplication of resources and effort. Integrating effor and content from a variety of sources has the potential to create wide-rangin network resources of major significance.

As working patterns and lifestyles change, there will be increasing expecta tion for *access* to library services to be available 24 hours a day, seven days week, from home, school, work and the cybercafé.

When books can arrive through the post a day after you ordered them fron an online bookshop, when national, international and regional newspapers ar available at the click of a mouse and you can find out the opening times of museum that you plan to visit 200 miles away, many people are going to need compelling reason to visit the website of their local library, let alone trek dow to their local branch library (if they can make it between 2 and 5pm, Tuesda to Friday, when it's open!). Regular Internet users already have their favourit sites where they will go to satisfy their information needs, be it for travel information from Railtrack or the latest story lines from 'EastEnders'. Public libraries will need to raise their profile and to be recognized as the *first point of call* for information needs.

For many people without the privilege of easy access to the Internet for personal use, the public library should be the obvious place to go if they want to search the web. However, with the growing popularity of cybercafés, with their long opening hours and competitive prices, the public library does have a major competitor in the battle to be seen as the *universal entry-point* to the digital age.

Developing online services – things to think about

The amount of material available on the Internet is enormous and will increase. Creating web pages is relatively easy, providing a form or *context* for that information is less so. The programmes that we have chosen to highlight above support projects that are concerned with much more than simply making information available electronically. They are attempting to organize and deliver resources in a meaningful way. This holistic approach, where the basic unit of information or resource is the starting-point for building 'experiences' around it, is exemplified by many public libraries' local history projects. *Knowsley Local History*[24] is a DCMS/Wolfson Challenge Fund project. It has taken over 500 local photographs and developed a seamless presentation recording the area's people and heritage. The photographs have been augmented through the inclusion of Ordnance Survey maps, artefacts from a local museum, audio interviews with local people and details taken from tithe maps held at the Lancashire Record Office.

Systems need to be future-proofed as far as possible if they are to be *sustainable*. Resources need to conform to technical standards and best practice in design should be followed. The Government has published guidelines for public sector websites.[25] The purpose of these is to promote excellence in public sector sites, through good management and good design. They include detailed technical standards for website construction and management to ensure usability and accessibility.

As more organizations and sectors collaborate, the *interoperability* of systems becomes increasingly important. The Interoperability Focus[26] based at UKOLN, works on a range of issues including the Z39.50 standard for information retrieval, metadata, distributed library systems and public library networking. The project also has a special interest in moving beyond the library sphere, to encompass museums, archives and other aspects of the cultural heritage.

As well as technical sustainability, services initially developed from project funding have to consider ways of sustaining maintenance and development in the long term. *Income generation*, while not the primary reason for the existence of a web presence for public sector services, is, for the reason explained above, an important aspect of online service provision. One way to satisfy the twin objectives of providing a public service free at the point of use to all while generating a modest amount of revenue, is by providing a range of access levels to resources. *SCRAN,*[27] a searchable archive of Scotland's history and culture, for example, provides free access to thumbnail images of its cultural artefacts while images of much higher resolution of the same objects can be viewed by those wishing to pay a premium.

A series of issue papers[28] is being produced by UKOLN, EARL and the Library Association to assist public library authorities shape and develop their own public access strategies to network resources and establish clearly defined roles for library services at the heart of public network developments.

Conclusion

The advent of the Internet has effectively removed the walls from the public library. They are now able to provide a 'stock' that extends far beyond what is held on their shelves. Managing this and providing a path through it for their users is the challenge that public librarians face at the turn of the century.

Public libraries are credited with extending literacy and educational opportunities to the masses via the printed medium at the beginning of the last century. At the beginning of this century, the challenges are the same, but the medium has changed.

References

1 Library and Information Commission, *New library: the people's network*, Library and Information Commission, 1997, also available at: **http://www.lic.gov.uk/publications/policyreports/newlibrary/index.html**
2 The Prime Minister and the Minister for the Cabinet Office, *Modernising*

Government, Stationery Office, 1999, also available at:
http://www.citu.gov.uk/moderngov/whitepaper/

3 *Our information age: the Government's vision*, Great Britain, Central Office of Information, 1998, also available at:
http://www.number-10.gov.uk/default.asp?PageId=1590

4 *NHS Direct Online*, available at:
http://www.nelh.nhs.uk/nhs_direct_online.htm

5 *BBC History 2000*, available at:
http://www.bbc.co.uk/history/events.shtml

6 Eggington, B, The first 'clicks-and-mortar' company, *BBC News*, available at:
http://news2.thls.bbc.co.uk/hi/english/business/newsid_597000/597388.stm

7 *People's Network Online*, available at:
http://www.lic.gov.uk/pno/

8 *New Opportunities Fund*, available at:
http://www.nof.org.uk/

9 *nof-digitisation programme*, available at:
http://www.nof.org.uk/tempdigit/index.html

10 *National Grid for Learning*, available at:
http://www.ngfl.gov.uk/

11 *24 hour museum*, available at:
http://www.24hourmuseum.org.uk/

12 *UfI/learndirect*, available at:
http://www.ufiltd.co.uk/

13 *Heritage Lottery Fund*, available at:
http://www.hlf.org.uk/

14 *Access to Archives Project*, available at:
http://www.pro.gov.uk/a2a/news.htm

15 *A netful of jewels: new museums and the learning age*, available at:
http://www.s-keene.dircon.co.uk/netful/

16 *European Commission's Information Society Technologies*, available at:
http://www.cordis.lu/ist/

17 *Electronic Libraries Programme*, available at:
http://www.ukoln.ac.uk/services/elib/

18 *SOSIG*, available at:
http://www.sosig.ac.uk/

19 *ADAM*, available at:
http://www.adam.ac.uk/
20 *OMNI*, available at:
http://www.omni.ac.uk/
21 *Resource Discovery Network*, available at:
http://www.rdn.ac.uk/
22 Further information about the *Distributed National Electronic Resource (DNER)* can be found at:
http://www.jisc.ac.uk/pub99/dner_vision.html
23 *DCMS/Wolfson Public Libraries Challenge Fund.* Information available on the DCMS website at:
http://www.culture.gov.uk/heritage/
24 *Knowsley Local History*, available at:
http://history.knowsley.gov.uk/
25 *Government guidelines for public sector websites*, available at:
http://www.iagchampions.gov.uk/guidelines/websites/websites.html
26 *Interoperability Focus*, available at:
http://www.ukoln.ac.uk/interop-focus/
27 *SCRAN*, available at:
http://www.scran.ac.uk/
28 *EARL Networked Services Policy Taskgroup*, in conjunction with UKOLN and the LA have published a number of papers that are available at:
http://www.earl.org.uk/taskgroups/policy/issue.htm

Glossary

applet A small **Java** program that can be embedded in an **HTML** page.

archie Utility that maintains a searchable database of the contents of **file archive** sites.

ASCII (American Standard Code for Information Interchange) Standard way of encoding characters, numbers and symbols. Plain text files are sometimes referred to as ASCII.

authentication A process, often using user names and passwords, to verify that users have the right to a particular service, such as one to which a university subscribes.

bandwidth Strictly the difference (measured in Hz), between the highest and lowest frequencies of a transmission, but used loosely to refer to the transmission capacity of the lines that carry the Internet's electronic traffic. The bandwidth will vary on different parts of the network, for example the transatlantic section has much less capacity than many local networks.

binary Notation using only the digits 0 and 1 – the simplest form used by a computer. Files retrieved by **FTP** may often be in binary.

Boolean Boolean logic is the use of 'operators' (words) like AND, OR, NOT and NEAR to specify the relationship between a combination of words to be searched for in a file or database

browser Software to view **world wide web** documents. Examples include Netscape Navigator and Microsoft Internet Explorer for graphical use, and Lynx for text only.

cache A temporary storage of web pages so that subsequent requests for the same pages do not have to go to the original location, so reducing long distance **network traffic**. A cache may be just on your machine, at your institution storing pages accessed by any users, or a national service.

CGI (Common Gateway Interface) CGI is a method used by web pages to communicate with programs run on the web **server**, for example, putting the content of a form into an **e-mail** message, or searching a database.

client A program on your computer that is used to contact and obtain data from a **server**, often across a great distance. A web **browser** is a client.

compression Procedures to pack files into a smaller size to reduce storag requirements and speed up transfer across networks. File names for com pressed files have extensions such as *.zip* and *.tar*. Compressed files must b uncompressed before they can be used.

conferencing Using **discussion lists** and **newsgroups** to communicat share information or debate particular subjects.

cookie A cookie is a short file put on your system by a **browser** whic includes information about your usage and helps the current use. For exam ple, it may include the information that you have logged into a passworde area already in the current session and don't need a second password check.

CWIS (**Campus Wide Information Service**) Information service for mem bers of a university or college. Now usually offered using the **world wid web**.

dataset Collection of numerical and bibliographic data made available fo searching across the Internet. UK examples are *BIDS* and *MIDAS*.

DCMS (Department for Culture, Media and Sport) UK Governmen department responsible for public libraries.

discussion list E-mail-based subject **conference**.

DNS (Domain Name System) The DNS is a service housed on a numbe of **servers** across the Internet which maintains a database for convertin between **domain names** and **IP addresses**. This allows users to specif remote computers by host names rather than numerical IP addresses.

domain name Unique alphabetic representation of a computer's locatio on the Internet. Compare **IP address**.

download To transfer a file, image, software or other material from a remot computer to your own.

EARL The EARL consortium of UK public libraries works to promote th role of public libraries in providing networked library and information ser- vices.

e-mail (electronic mail) System which enables messages to be sent from one person's computer (or space on a central computer) to another.

FAQ (**Frequently Asked Question**) Common questions and answers about a particular topic are often collected in a FAQ file, which is updated as nec- essary and reissued periodically, commonly on a **newsgroup**.

file archive Collection of files – such as software, numerical data, texts – that can be retrieved by **FTP**.

irewall A machine with special security precautions which is used to prevent unauthorized external access to sensitive information held by an organization.

TP (File Transfer Protocol) A standard **protocol** (and an application) which permits files to be copied from one computer to another, regardless of file format or operating system.

if (Graphic Interchange Format) A common format for image files, especially suitable for images containing large areas of the same colour, for example a logo, and for line drawings. gif format files can be used for photographs but **JPEG** is preferred.

opher Utility that organizes information in hierarchical ways and also allows users to retrieve and view text information from **servers** on the Internet. Now little used.

GUI (Graphical User Interface) A graphical way of using computers that involves using a mouse to make choices, rather than keying commands. Microsoft Windows and Netscape Navigator are examples.

ost A computer system which provides a service, such as **electronic mail** or access to a database.

HTML (HyperText Markup Language) The coding system used for creating documents on the **world wide web** that can be read using a **browser**.

HTTP (HyperText Transfer Protocol) The search and retrieval **protocol** used for transferring **HTML** documents.

hypermedia Electronic media – text, graphics, video, sound – linked to provide information.

hypertext Text that contains links to other text, allowing information to be retrieved non-sequentially.

Internet The worldwide collection of interconnected computer networks.

intranet A private network inside an organization that uses the same kinds of software, such as a web **browser** and **HTML** files, that you would find on the public **Internet**, but that is usually only for internal use. Thus some teaching or administrative material on university web systems may be restricted to that university only.

ICT (Information and Communication Technologies)

IP address Unique numeric representation of a computer's location on the Internet. It comprises four sets of numbers separated by periods. Compare **domain name**.

ISP (Internet Service Provider)

An organization that provides access to the Internet, usually for a fee.

JANET (Joint Academic Network) The computer network linking UK higher and further education institutions and research organizations.

Java A programming language that can be used to create applications such as animation and multimedia for web pages.

Javascript A script language (with little in common with **Java**) developed by Netscape for writing short programs embedded in a web page.

JPEG (Joint Photographic Experts Group) JPEG is a common format for image files and is best for full-colour or grey-scale photographic-type digital images.

LAN (Local Area Network) A computer network limited to the immediate area, usually the same building or organization.

LIC (Library and Information Commission) The public body responsible for advising the UK Government on all issues relating to the library and information sector. The LIC (and the Museums & Galleries Commission) were replaced on 1 April 2000 with **Resource**, The Council for Museums, Archives and Libraries.

Listserv A common **utility** used to manage **discussion lists** on the Internet.

Lynx A text-only web **browser**.

Mailbase The organization which manages and promotes the use of **discussion lists** for UK higher education.

MIMAS (Manchester InforMation and Associated Services) A service for UK higher education providing economic and social statistics, bibliographic databases and electronic journals.

MIME (Multipurposes Internet Mail Extensions) The standard for attaching non-text files to standard Internet mail messages. Non-text files include graphics, spreadsheets, formatted word-processor documents, sound files, etc. It is also used by web **servers** to identify the files – such as sound, video, etc, they are sending to **browsers**.

mirror A mirror site is an exact copy of a web or **FTP** site in another geographical location so as to improve local access. Popular sites may have mirrors in various parts of the world.

Modem (MOdulator, DEModulator) A device that connects a computer to a phone line, allowing the computer to talk to other computers through the phone system.

MPEG (Moving Pictures Experts Group) A format that defines the standard of performance in audio and video playback.

Netscape The company producing Netscape Navigator, a widely used graphical **browser** for the **world wide web**. The browser itself is usually referred to just as Netscape.

network traffic The flow of information in local, national and international networks. Excessive network traffic leads to slower responses to information requests.

newsgroups The hierarchically arranged collection of topic areas in **Usenet**.

newsreader Software needed to read **newsgroups**. It may be included in a web **browser**.

NISS (National Information Services and Systems) The organization providing the *NISS Information Gateway* service for UK education.

NOF (New Opportunities Fund) A National Lottery distributor awarding grants to health, education and environment projects throughout the UK.

OPAC (Online Public Access Catalogue) An acronym commonly used to describe a computerized library catalogue.

PDF (Page Description Format) A format that allows much more controlled layout of text and graphics on a web page than conventional **HTML** does. It requires a **browser** plug-in to see a web page in PDF format. A proprietary format from Adobe.

People's Network The project spearheading the delivery of lifelong learning initiatives through public libraries. One aim of the project is to connect all public libraries to the Information Superhighway by the end of 2002 wherever possible.

plug-in A (usually small) piece of optional software that adds features to a larger program. Web **browsers** like **Netscape** Navigator use plug-ins for multimedia files, compressed text, sound, etc. As **browsers** develop, such features will become standard.

POP (Point of Presence, also **Post Office Protocol)** A geographic location where a network can be connected, often with dial-up phone lines. Post Office Protocol refers to the way e-mail software gets mail from a mail server.

port A connection to a computer system, through which data can be exchanged.

protocol A well-defined set of data-exchange rules that apply to communication between computer systems.

Resource, The Council for Museums, Archives and Libraries A nee strategic agency working with and for museums, archives and libraries throughout the UK.

search engine Software that searches a database. Commonly used to describe services that search the content of the **world wide web**.

server A computer which provides software and services across a local, national or international network.

spam The Internet version of junk mail. Spamming is sending the same message to a large number of people, mailing lists or **newsgroups**, usually to advertise something. It is not a practice that is encouraged.

telnet A standard **protocol** (and an application) that permits a user to log on to a remote computer system.

tool Another word for **utility**.

UKOLN (the UK Office for Library and Information Networking) UKOLN is a national focus of expertise in network information management. It provides policy, research and awareness services to the UK library and information communities.

Unix A computer operating system that is commonly used on machines offering Internet services.

URL (Uniform Resource Locator) Standard naming/addressing system for files on the Internet.

Usenet Worldwide **conferencing** system comprising thousands of **newsgroups** on a huge range of subjects.

utility A program for a particular small task, such as managing **e-mail** or creating **HTML** text.

virus A small program that is designed to create mischief or damage on computers. Viruses can be downloaded with other software, found on the disks on the covers of magazines, or obtained in other unintended ways. Your computer should have an anti-virus program to detect viruses.

VRML (Virtual Reality Modelling Language) The programming language used to create virtual reality applications across the Internet.

VT100 A standard for terminal display that is usually needed for **telnet** connections.

WAIS (Wide-Area Information Server) A means of indexing and searching text files on the Internet. Less commonly used than it was.

www (world wide web) The part of the Internet consisting of **hypermedia**, and needing a **browser** to view its pages.

Z39.50 A standard for connecting library computers and databases regardless of hardware and software.

For extensive glossaries of terms see:

Glossary of Internet terms
http://www.delphi.com/navnet/glossary

ILC Glossary of Internet Terms
http://www.matisse.net/files/glossary.html

ndex

'his is an index mainly to concepts, issues, techniques and to resources by
ʏpe or subject. Specific Internet resources are not included.